Acrylic on canvas
130cm x 80cm
New York City, 2004

*CELEBRATING
AHMED MORSI
EGYPTIAN POET
AND ARTIST
PAGE 78*

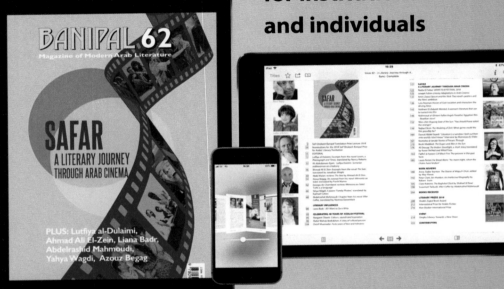

Dying in a Mother Tongue

BY ROJA CHAMANKAR
TRANSLATED BY BLAKE ATWOOD

This vivid and lyrical collection introduces English-language readers for the first time to one of the most acclaimed Iranian poets of her generation.

5½ x 8½ inches, 70 pages • $16.00 paperback

At last this contemporary voice from Iran gets introduced to English readers in translations worthy of her verse.
—ROGER SEDARAT
Queens College, City University of New York

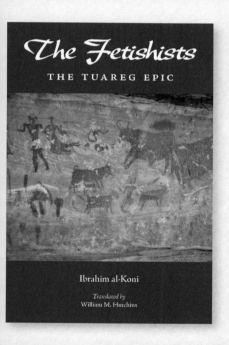

The Fetishists

BY IBRAHIM AL-KONI
TRANSLATED BY WILLIAM M. HUTCHINS

This epic novel of Tuareg culture in the Saharan Desert is considered the greatest work of Ibrahim al-Koni, one of the most prolific and important writers in Arabic today.

6 x 9 inches, 454 pages
$30.00 paperback

UNIVERSITY OF TEXAS PRESS

800.252.3206 | www.utexaspress.com

The Forum for Arab and International Relations

The Forum for Arab and International Relations

Announces its fifth international conference on

Translation and the Problematics of Crosscultural Understanding (5)

to be held in Doha, Qatar, 11-12 December 2018.

The conference coincides with the fourth prize winning ceremony of **the Sheikh Hamad Award for Translation and International Understanding**

The topics of interest include:

- The problematics of Arabic/German translations.

- Translation and its problematic relationship with authority and censorship.

- What do/should we translate?

- Translation and the problematics of reception (Reception theory, practice and mechanisms; the Arab-Islamic culture and its reception of Greek thought; Western culture and its reception of Arab-Islamic thought; the Arab-Islamic culture and its reception of modern western thought; reception and the rivalries of precedence in scientific and artistic discoveries; stages of reception and the dialectics of shock-rejection-recognition-acceptance-renewal-creativity).

- Modern/Contemporary philosophical thought and the problematics of translation.

- Otherness and forms of its presence in translation (Otherness as a project; what is "the other" and how do we come to understand her/him/them; aspects of the relationship with "the other."

- Translating the social sciences.

- Translating religious and culturally-specific texts.

- Literary translation (rendering modernist English poetry into Arabic: Yeats, Eliot, Pound).

- The problematics of translating biographies/ autobiographies, memoires, histories.

- The image of the Arab and Islamic world conveyed by translators to other languages and cultures: Is it a reflection of the unfortunate reality or a disguised cultural bias?

- Corpus: its significance, uses and techniques in translation and terminology.

- Towards establishing a referential body to sanction translations and protect the rights of translators.

For more information:

Phone: +974 44080451   E-mail: info@fairforum.org

Website: www.fairforum.org 🅧 🅕 fairforum

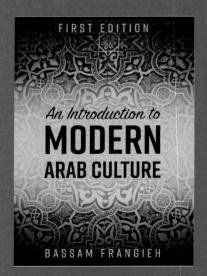

FIRST EDITION

An Introduction to
MODERN
ARAB CULTURE

BASSAM FRANGIEH

An Introduction to Modern Arab Culture

by Bassam Frangieh

introduces readers to aspects of Arab culture that create a unique tapestry of identity, experience, and history. The book is well suited to courses in Middle East culture and history, politics, thought, literature, religion, and language, and courses in sociology, anthropology, and cultural studies.

Bassam Frangieh, PhD, is a professor of Arabic at Claremont McKenna College and a scholar of contemporary Arabic literature and culture. An Introduction to Modern Arab Culture is published by Cognella Academic Publishing, USA, 2019.
ISBN: 978-1-5165-2629-1
Paperback, 434 pages,
USD85.95

cognella®
ACADEMIC PUBLISHING

Ahmed Morsi
The Black Fish
Acrylic on canvas
152cm x 132cm
New York City, 1984

BANIPAL

Magazine of Modern Arab Literature

Banipal magazine, founded in 1998, takes its name from Ashurbanipal (668–627 BC), the last great king of Assyria and patron of the arts, whose outstanding achievement was to assemble in his capital Nineveh, Mesopotamia, from all over his empire, the first systematically organised library in the ancient Middle East. The thousands of clay tablets of Sumerian, Babylonian and Assyrian writings included the famous Mesopotamian epics of the Creation, the Flood, and Gilgamesh, many folk tales, fables, proverbs, prayers and omen texts.

Source: *Encyclopaedia Britannica*

PUBLISHER: Margaret Obank

EDITOR: Samuel Shimon

CONTRIBUTING EDITORS
Fadhil al-Azzawi, Peter Clark, Raphael Cohen, Bassam Frangieh, Camilo Gómez-Rivas, William M Hutchins, Adil Babikir, Imad Khachan, Khaled Mattawa, Clare Roberts, Mariam al-Saedi, Anton Shammas, Paul Starkey

CONSULTING EDITORS
Etel Adnan, Roger Allen, Issa J Boullata, Isabella Camera d'Afflitto, Humphrey Davies, Hartmut Fähndrich, Ibrahim Farghali, Naomi Shihab Nye, Nancy Roberts, Susannah Tarbush

EDITORIAL ASSISTANTS: Annamaria Basile, Rosie Maxton, Maureen O'Rourke, Hannah Somerville, Valentina Viene

ADDITIONAL TRANSLATION: Adil Babikir, Najlaa Eltom

COVER PAINTING: Ahmed Morsi

LAYOUT: Banipal Publishing

WEBSITE: www.banipal.co.uk

EDITOR: editor@banipal.co.uk

PUBLISHER: margaret@banipal.co.uk

INQUIRIES: info@banipal.co.uk

SUBSCRIPTIONS: subscribe@banipal.co.uk

ADDRESS: 1 Gough Square, London EC4A 3DE

PRINTED BY Marston Book Services
Milton Park, Abingdon OX14 4SB

Photographs not accredited have been donated, photographers unknown.

BANIPAL 63 – The 100 Best Arabic Novels

BANIPAL, ISSN 1461-5363, is published three times a year by Banipal Publishing, 1 Gough Square, London EC4A 3DE

Supported using public funding by
ARTS COUNCIL ENGLAND
LOTTERY FUNDED

www.banipal.co.uk

EDITORIAL

This issue of Banipal magazine is a feast of literary fiction, poetry, essays, book reviews and paintings, opening in surprising colour. Do let us know what you think.

The title feature **The 100 best Arabic novels** is a new up-to-date list in response to the greatly increased popularity of novels in the Arab world. The introduction explains how it was prepared and nominations ranked. To whet your appetite, here are the first five: *Season of Migration to the North* by Tayeb Salih, the *Cairo Trilogy* by Naguib Mahfouz, *For Bread Alone* by Mohamed Choukri, *The Secret Life of Saeed The Pessoptimist* by Emile Habiby and *Children of the Alley*, also by Naguib Mahfouz.

We present a feature on Iraqi writer and academic **Hayat Sharara** who tragically lost her life to suicide after decades of struggling against and suffering the tyranny of the Ba'athist regime and the later barbaric western sanctions. Her posthumously published novel *When the Days Grow Dark* excerpted below is a lament for the city of Baghdad by the first-person narrator, who is, like Hayat Sharara, a university teacher. He can only talk in whispers, even to himself, and is haunted by a nauseous fear that no one is immune from, and that "even stuck to their clothes". The daily life continues relentlessly, with people, worn down by constant orders, daily humiliations and intimidations, facing no alternative but to go along with the culture of orders . . . that had to be obeyed.

The striking front cover painting is by Egyptian poet and artist **Ahmed Morsi**, whose paintings and poems are celebrated in this issue. The poems, selected from his *Photos from the New York Album*, are paintings in words that become mini films – driving to Manhattan, or in scenes with neighbours in apartment blocks.

We present works by three further Egyptian writers. In a chapter from the novel *To Be Loved by Jihan*, by the late **Mekkawi Said**, we meet a shy young man who is unsuccessful in getting to know Jihan and so tries to attract the attention of the beautiful Reem, a TV presenter, to the envy of his friend Emad. The short story by paediatrician and author **Azza Rashad**, entitled *Prickly Jasmine*, is about two sisters growing up, with beautiful descriptions of their comings and goings: Jasmine is always taking photos on her mobile phone and Reem has a secret boyfriend Karim, whom she is eventually allowed to marry. The three poems of **Girgis Shukry**, poet and cultural journalist, are a combination of imaginative musings about what poetry is all about and contemplative observations the passage of life – "I'll put the future in the fridge / beside the tomatoes /that will be best / and throw the past down the lavatory."

We honour the memory of Syrian author **Hanna Mina**, the indefatigable pioneer of the Arabic novel. He has left a lasting legacy in his numerous works of a passionate and genuine rage "against colonialism, corruption and injustice across the Middle East" that is greatly needed today.

Rounding off the issue are a number of book reviews that will give readers plenty of ideas for books to buy, or borrow from the library. In one, of Syrian poet Nouri al-Jarrah's first collection in English translation *A Boat to Lesbos* (Banipal Books, 2018) fellow poet **Ruth Padel** writes of his "unforgettable lyrics".

Hayat Sharara

Ahmed Morsi

Mekkawi Said

Azza Rashad

Girgis Shukry

Ahmed Morsi: The Fish Eye
Acrylic on canvas 213cm x 127 cm
New York City 2012

Hanan al-Shaykh

Abdelrahman Munif

Gamal el-Ghitani

Remembering an excellent Iraqi intellectual

On August 1, 1997 our dreams of a reunion were dealt a fatal blow with the tragic news that both Hayat and her daughter Maha had committed suicide. Hayat left behind the city she had loved most, with its towering palm trees and orange trees spreading their fragrance along the banks of the Tigris.

Balkis Sharara

HAYAT
SHARARA
1935 – 1997

BALKIS SHARARA

She felt she was under surveillance at the university

N ajaf is a unique city like no other in the world, except perhaps India's Varanasi. Najaf is two cities: one for the dead and another for the living. However, the dividing line between the two melts away sometimes and they become an undistinguishable one. The city of the dead is not entirely empty of living human beings. Scores of people from the city of the living do come down during the day to perform funeral rituals. Coffins pour in from every corner of the Islamic World, and voices of bereaved relatives are heard around the city while ghosts of the dead loom on the horizon, lending it an air of muffled panic.

On its part, the city of the living is not entirely empty of the dead. Coffins carried on shoulders are lined up at the central court of Imam Ali Mosque in preparation for funeral prayers. The interaction of the living and the dead is continuous. Funeral rituals mix with the clamour of children playing in a corner of the vast courtyard, and the chatter of women wrapped in their traditional abayas sitting around tea samovars. The mosque is the only escape for the children and women from loneliness at home and the boredom of the dim, winding alleyways.

The city of the living is engulfed in a mythical aura. It is a magnet for Shiite Muslims, and the corridors of its ancient mosques are teeming with students who come from South Lebanon, Iran, and India to learn Arabic and for Islamic studies from the city's religious scholars.

Another aspect of Najaf is its thriving cultural activity. It is home to many newspapers and magazines – such as *Al-Hatif*, *Al-Hadhara*, *Al-Ghari*, and *Al-Bayan*, which have played a leading role in social reform. It is also home to iconic writers and poets like Mohammad

Mahdi al-Jawahiri, Ali al-Sharqi, Jaafar al-Khalili, and Said Saleh — and from Lebanon Hussain Mrouwa and Mohammed Sharara.

It was in this environment that Hayat was born in the old neighbourhood of the city in 1935. She demonstrated significant literary talent from an early age. She developed a strong passion for modern poetry, thanks to my father, who used to recite poetry almost daily, and we stored many of these in our memory. Besides, he was a great help to us in improving our Arabic language proficiency as he spoke standard Arabic even in our daily conversations. Hayat showed high talent in memorizing complete poetry collections and proved herself a staunch competitor of my father in the poetry competitions held within the family.

When we moved to Baghdad in the mid-1940s, our house became a meeting place for many poets, littérateurs, and thinkers of divergent political affiliations. During those weekly meetings, Hayat sat in a corner of the room, carrying in her tiny hands a notebook where she wrote down the new poems recited, little knowing that those were the seeds of a new current of Arabic poetry. A major

. . . Hayat was born in the old neighbourhood of Najaf in 1935

Mohhamad Mahdi al-Jawahiri   *Badr Shakir al-Sayyab*

theme of discussion during those meetings was renewal of poetic forms and adopting a free verse style.

Badr Shakir al-Sayyab and Lamia Abbas Amara were constantly present at those gatherings, which also attracted other names such as Mohammad Mahdi al-Jawahiri, Hussain Mrouwa, Nazik al-Malaika, Akram al-Watari, Buland al-Haidari, and Mohsin al-Amin. Nazik came most of the time in the company of her father Sadiq al-Malaika, and sometimes with her brother Nizar.

The three that had the most profound influence on us were Badr, Lamia, and Nazik. Badr was particularly wrathful at the prevalent sociopolitical conditions. He deserted his well-to-do family when he joined the Iraqi Communist Party. That revolutionary mood left its mark on his early poems. Skinny, dark skinned, with large, protruding ears, a big nose, tiny eyes, and lips pushed forward by protruding teeth, al-Sayyab was not particularly good looking. Yet he was highly sensitive and compassionate, always fascinated by beauty in nature and women. He suffered a series of setbacks in his love affairs. He readily fell in love with girls, and would immediately compose poems in their praise but would lampoon them if they turned him down. He was excessively shy.

One of those girls who fascinated al-Sayyab was Lamia, his colleague at the High Institute of Teachers, who had inspired many of the poems he recited in her presence at the weekly gathering. She was aware of that and knew how to stoke his affection by her enigmatic glances. His love for Lamia was undisguised.

Lamia combined a smart personality and attractive appearance.

She was tall and slim, with wide black eyes, and beautiful black hair. Although she always wore a black dress, she was glimmering and full of vigour. Unlike al-Sayyab, she was an eloquent speaker, with a strong sense of satire. When she recited her poems, she skillfully used body language to fascinate her audience. Her poems were short and agile, with love being the underlying theme.

* * *

Lamia Abbas Amara

In 1949, which marked the first anniversary of the demonstrations that toppled the Portsmouth Treaty, martial law was imposed and the country drifted into a massive wave of arrests unprecedented since the movement of Rashid Ali al-Gaylani. Political parties were disbanded, newspapers were closed, and scores of intellectuals and politicians were arrested, among them my father and Uncle Murtadha. One night, police raided our home, searched all the rooms, rummaged through my father's library and confiscated many of his books and papers, including pictures of us with schoolmates during the funeral of the martyrs of the 1948 demonstrations against the Anglo-Iraqi Treaty. Our once joyful world was turned upside down. My father and Uncle Murtadha were taken to Abu Ghraib prison, along with leftist intellectuals such as al-Sayyab, al-Jawahiri, as well as opposition party leaders and university students.

Having experienced the injustice meted out to her family during part of her childhood, Hayat became a political activist in the prime of her youth, with an overwhelming zeal to fight oppression and injustice. These aspirations were captured in her (unpublished) novel *Wamidhu Barqin Ba'eed* (A Distant Glimmer), where she wrote: "If man manages to break the social bonds that throttle him like thick ropes, he will transform into a completely different person. We are

Nazik al-Malaika

accused and convicted in the court of society and denied the right to defend our case."

The Iraqi Communist Party spearheaded the struggle against social injustice. At a time when it was in dire need of young, committed Iraqis, it nominated Hayat, who was still under 17, to attend a peace conference held in Prague, Czechoslovakia, in 1952. Shortly after her departure, the "November Upheaval" erupted on November 23, 1952, demanding the abolition of the 1930 Treaty and amendment of the Election Law. The upheaval was triggered by the dismissal of four students from the College of Commerce, University of Baghdad. When demands for their return were turned down, the students took to the streets where they were joined by members of the public. The demonstrators were brutally confronted by police. A state of martial law was imposed and scores of leftist students and thinkers were arrested. My father went underground somewhere in Najaf. When police raided our home, they found no one but my 14-year-old brother Ibrahim, who was released only upon the intervention of Bahjat al-Attiyah, Director of Public Security, who was an acquaintance of my father but not happy with his political leanings. A court of martial law sentenced my father to one year in prison on account of his affiliation with Ansaar al-Salam (Heralds of Peace) and for publishing some articles.

* * *

Although she completed high school successfully and obtained her baccalaureate, Hayat did not gain admission to Baghdad University because she could not obtain a certificate of good conduct (CGD), which was used as a weapon against disloyal students, particularly leftists and communists, to deny them access to college education and employment. No wonder scores of high school graduates had to flee to Syria and Egypt. Hayat had no alternative but to leave for Syria.

Having arrived after the academic year had started in Syrian universities, she decided to go to Egypt where she enrolled at the English language department at Cairo University. In Egypt, she met many Iraqi students, amongst them her future husband Mohammad Saleh Smaisim, who had fled from the oppression of the Iraqi monarchy. Smaisim took good care of Hayat and their relation soon developed into a love affair but they had to postpone their engagement until they returned to Baghdad in 1958, after the 14th of July revolution. They had to wait until 1970 before they could get married, following her return from Moscow in 1968.

During her stay in Cairo, she spent most of her time reading in the quiet halls of the College of Law, away from the bustling corridors of the College of Arts, which attracted male students aspiring to meet female counterparts. At that time, students lived in segregated areas. Leftist and progressive students, for instance, never interacted with Ba'athists and Arab Nationalists. That dichotomy and inflexibility continued to haunt the political scene post the 1958 Revolution.

* * *

Upon her return from Cairo following the 14th of July revolution, Hayat joined the College of Art to complete her English language programme. However, she could not pursue her studies as diligently as she hoped because she was overburdened with onerous Communist Party assignments, which included mobilization of people for demonstrations, awareness-building, and attending extensive Party meetings. She had to work extensive hours without rest, even when she was sick. These pressures had their toll on her health.

Although chaos and atrocities continued during that period, Iraq did see some degree of tolerance. Opposition parties, including Arab Nationalists, Ba'athists, Communists, and liberals, were permitted to publish newspapers and magazines. The opposition press was outspoken in its criticism of the policies of Abd Al-Karim Qasim, while *Sawt al-Sha'ab* (The Voice of the People), a mouthpiece of the Communist Party, waged violent tirades against the "Enemies of the Revolution".

When Abd Al-Karim Qasim started to move closer to the centre and right, veering away from the left and the Communist Party, the Ba'ath Party emerged as a significant force. In association with the Nationalists, they successfully played on the public phobia of communism to isolate and undermine the leftists and communists. As part of their campaign, they accused the communists of desecrating the holy Qur'an, which prompted angry demonstrations demanding liquidation of "the infidels". The battle between the two camps escalated during the trade union elections, which culminated in the Nationalists/Ba'athists taking over.

The Qasim administration grew so weak that lethal assaults on the President's advocates became a daily occurrence. Qasim himself barely escaped a daylight attempt on his life. On their part, the Ba'athists developed into a formidable political force, and when their second coup attempt brought them back to power in August 1968, they adopted a more tolerant policy, offering clemency to all leftists, liberals, and communists, and reinstating them into their jobs.

It was in that period that Hayat returned to Baghdad, after obtaining a doctoral degree in Russian literature from Moscow University. She had to stay for an extra year beyond her five-year scholarship in order to write her thesis on "Tolstoy as an Artist". Because she declined to cooperate with the Communist Party officials looking after the Iraqi students, the Soviet authorities refused to issue her a grant for that extra year, and she had to work as a freelance translator with the TASS News Agency, and had to sell most of her clothes in order to complete the final year.

Back in Baghdad, she steered away from political activity and took up a position as a lecturer in Russian literature at Baghdad University's Faculty of Languages. Two years later, she married Dr Mohammad Saleh Smaisim.

* * *

Ba'athist rule was ruthless, particularly in their first years, when scores of people were hanged in Tahrir Square. However, it was only those perceived as a real threat who were targeted.

After the 1973 war, Iraq received an intensive influx of petrodollars, but most of the funds were spent on building Iraq's military might, while very little went to infrastructure, culture, and healthcare.

* * *

Although Ahmad Hassan al-Bakr was the President, it was Vice-President Saddam Hussain who was the de facto ruler. Saddam used to go on tours across Iraq and distribute gifts, including fridges and TV sets, to people. Such acts raised his popularity.

The so-called Tabbayyah, referring to Iraqis who did not hold Ottoman passports, were expelled on the grounds that they were Iranians, although many of them were Arabs who did not speak Persian. They were stripped of their money and ejected over the Iraqi borders. In many cases, families were split. A wife who had an Ottoman passport would be allowed to stay with her children while the husband, who had no such passport, would be expelled. Tabbayyah covered a large cross section of Iraqi society.

The Ba'athists continued to tighten their grip on the country. Significant privileges, including access to undergraduate and post-graduate scholarships abroad, were offered exclusively to the Party's cadres to the exclusion of all others. As part of the Party's policy to turn the teaching sector into an exclusive territory for the Ba'athists, Hayat was asked to join the [Ba'ath] Party if she valued her university job. When she refused, she was transferred to the Ministry of Industry to work as an interpreter on a Russian project.

* * *

In September 1980, when the war with Iran broke out, and death spread its wings over Iraq, Hayat wrote to me: "Pain and tragedy have become part of life. We are caught in a crazy dilemma that reminds me of the situation in Lebanon. Yet, running away is no relief to me. I am deeply rooted here, in this very land that keeps boiling and raging with death and destruction but never kills our hopes. As long as the flame of hope is still alive in my heart, I should be fine."

As the war continued to consume one generation after another, students grew so scared of being sent to the battlefield that they deliberately performed badly enough in their exams to ensure they did not pass to the next year and thus stayed at the university for as long as they possibly could. Venting her frustration at this situation, she once wrote to me, "Students have lost the motive to learn. Our efforts are worthless. Learning has become a losing business."

Later, however, she found some excuse for those students when she realized the troubles they faced upon return from the training camps. "They lost the faculty of imagining and dreaming, and with that all their once blossoming hopes and ambitions died. The present is falling apart before their very eyes, its debris falling on both the past and future."

Despite the ongoing war, that period proved to be highly productive for Hayat. As she mentioned in her letters to me, she wrote several articles on poetry and theatre and started translating some novels and some difficult poems that had not been translated before.

* * *

During the 1980s, Hayat tried hard to obtain a passport in order to visit relatives in Lebanon and to find publishers for her work. Only after ten years of unsuccessful attempts did she finally get approval. She wrote to me on February 13, 1990: "At last visiting you has become possible. The travel ban has been lifted and once we heard the news we started to dream of travelling to neighbouring countries. Life without dreams is barren and dull. We had a big celebration at the college."

Hayat went to London with her two daughters to spend summer with our sister Mariam. However, with the outbreak of the Gulf War, she returned home at the beginning of the academic year.

By the end of 1991, Hayat had another problem to face. A new rule was issued banning females under 45 years from travelling abroad unless accompanied by a first-degree male guardian. The ra-

tionale given for the ban was that some Iraqi girls became professional prostitutes in order to make a living abroad. "Now Maha and
Zeinab cannot travel without a male guardian," Hayat wrote in one
of her letters. "I don't know if we are going to overcome this."

* * *

Having failed to publish her short stories, Hayat experimented
with the novel. "I am currently writing a long story," she told me.
"I started only two months ago and am not sure when I will finish
it. But I am not in a hurry, though; publishing it is unlikely anyway,
given the high cost both in Iraq and abroad. I don't know what the
novel will look like in the end. It is guiding me, not the other way
round. I might finish it by the beginning of summer. It is a new experience. I don't know how it will end up, but it is an interesting
experience I am totally engrossed in. It has become part of my life."

The economic embargo started to weigh heavily on the Iraqi people. Basic consumer goods and medicines disappeared from the markets and Iraq returned to the rationing system that had prevailed
during World War II. Hayat wrote to me in early 1994: "Eating
chocolates has become a rare occurrence and a surreal experience."

In 1994, her daughter Maha graduated from university and started
to look for a job. Although she successfully passed an interview for
a job at the Ministry of Oil, her appointment was blocked by the
Minister, citing two reasons: she was not part of the Ba'ath Party,
and her mother was Hayat Sharara.

Hayat was profoundly offended. She wrote to me: "Things have
changed tremendously, Balkis. We are in a critical situation. I want
Maha and Zeinab to become independent because they have no sup-
port apart from me. But things may change in future and job op-
portunities would become available. We hope things will get better
and life return to normal after the embargo is lifted."

But things only got worse. Apart from daily hardships, Hayat felt
she was under surveillance at the university. In her novel *Idha al-
Ayaam Aghsaqat* (When the Days Grow Dark), she wrote: "Training
yourself to avoid slips of the tongue and learning the whispered language that has become the rule." She asked me to stop sending letters to her university postal address because several letters had been
opened by the college security officer.

. . . Thus, it was in the historic city of Najaf that Hayat came to this world, and it was in Baghdad, the city of peace, that her life came to an end.

In the face of continuous harassment, Hayat felt she could no longer continue in her teaching job. She applied for retirement but her request was turned down. Due to her prolonged absence from college, she was considered to have resigned and accordingly deprived of her benefits for 26 years of service.

That stifling climate left her with no alternative but to think of leaving her country. Although Iraqis historically stuck to their soil, conditions deteriorated to a point where migration became the aspiration of every one.

Hayat appealed to the President [Saddam Hussein] for permission to travel along with her two daughters. The authorities returned the appeal to her and instructed her to rewrite it in a submissive tone. She dismissed that as an insult and refused to do so.

As a result of the economic embargo, intellectuals lived in isolation from the outside world since books and magazines were banned, as were cassettes and videos. I was terribly worried about Hayat and when I expressed my worries to her, she sent me a consoling letter. "Don't worry about us. We spend a good part of our time reading. In the evenings we walk leisurely on the roof and watch the sun as it sets behind palm trees."

Hayat found great relief in writing. "I am happy to discover that I have not lost my writing talent," she said in one of her last letters. She said she was finalizing her latest novel *Idha al-Ayaam Aghsaqat*, about her experience at the university.

On August 1, 1997, our dreams of a reunion were dealt a fatal blow with the tragic news that both Hayat and her daughter Maha had committed suicide. Hayat left behind the city she had loved most, with its towering palm trees and orange trees spreading their fragrance along the banks of the Tigris.

She left behind a different city that shared little with the one she had known and loved. A city reeking of foul sewers and dead bodies on the streets, where mosquitoes, flies, stray dogs and cats, and barefooted children feasted on heaps of garbage everywhere across the city. A wounded city, inhabited by dead bodies in motion. Yet, the sad looks of the hungry and terrified people concealed a silent revolution building up.

Thus, it was in the historic city of Najaf that Hayat came to this world, and it was in Baghdad, the city of peace, that her life came to an end.

Translated by Adil Babikir

The excerpts above were selected from the 80-page introduction to *Idha al-Ayyam Aghsaqat* (When the Days Grow Dark), the last novel of Hayat Sharara, published posthumously by al-Muassassa al-Arabiya lil-Dirassat wal-Nashr, Amman, 2000

FADHIL CHALABI

Heroic outcry against injustice

S uicide had been a rare occurrence in Iraq until the country was plunged into the devastating wars orchestrated by the ruling regime. However, in the ensuing socioeconomic collapse that brought poverty and misery to a large part of the population, cases of suicide became commonplace, particularly among the middle class. Many parents just could not tolerate seeing their families in the throes of poverty and want, with their daughters selling their bodies to earn enough to eat.

Many might read Hayat Sharara's suicide in that context. She had been plunged into despair after her benefits had been confiscated. To make things worse, her daughters were banned from travelling abroad under a bizarre law that prohibited women under 45 from going abroad except in the company of a first-degree male relative.

However, those who read Hayat's novel *Idha al-Ayyam Aghsaqat* (When the Days Grow Dark), and the rich introduction by her sister Balkis, might find clues to what had driven such a gifted writer to take her life at the peak of her intellectual powers. Indeed, she could have maintained her university job by simply joining the ranks of the ruling Ba'ath Party. But she was not one who would do anything at the expense of her dignity and self-respect. Similarly, she could have easily obtained permission to travel by submitting a plea to the authorities, but she did not do so because she firmly believed that travelling was a basic human right, not a favour from the Government.

In essence, her suicide was an outcry against a regime that had consistently targeted the human dignity, intellectual freedom, and livelihood of Iraqi intellectuals. It was particularly frustrating to watch how the elites were humiliated and downtrodden in a country

Hayat set her novel in a Baghdad university as the ideal place to highlight the ordeals of the intelligentsia

that had historically celebrated its intelligentsia and accorded them special status. University lecturers lost their independent voices. They had to chant with the chanters, join parades and military training exercises and even take part in actual battles to avoid unwanted scenarios such as dismissal, retirement, withdrawal of ration cards, or an even more horrible fate at the hands of intelligence elements.

Hayat set her novel in a Baghdad university as the ideal place to highlight the ordeals of the intelligentsia – a place teeming with intelligence agents and informants from among both the students and faculty. With wiretaps and bugs placed everywhere, faculty members can only whisper to each other as "walls have ears". Students affiliated to the security organs, or to the ruling party, have the upper hand, and teachers have no choice but to give them high marks, regardless of their actual performance. The Dean, in military uniform, is often seen standing at the gate or swaggering around the corridors, spreading threats here and there, yelling at a lecturer who is five minutes late, rebuking another in a vulgar show of force.

Many lecturers are driven by fear to serve as informants for the intelligence

Hayat Sharara defending her PhD thesis in 1968

apparatus. One of those is Badri, who agrees to supply information about his relatives in order to distract the authorities from digging out his past association with an illicit political party. As a result, that brilliant scholar ends up an alcoholic.

The story of Dr Akram, an accomplished researcher, carries echoes of characters from George Orwell and Franz Kafka. His life is turned upside down when he is fired from his job for "treason", although the dismissal letter does not give any details. From then on, he is deserted by almost everyone, and those who wish to visit him do so only at dead of night since intelligence agents are keeping an eye on him. He runs his own car as a taxi, but the income he earns from that barely covers the cost of repairs and spare parts. After many unsuccessful attempts to earn a living, including a short-lived association with his brother in a grain store, he succumbs to despair and settles for a permanent association with arak.

The character of Dr Abboud takes a more dramatic turn, as he becomes mad after his dismissal. The pragmatic Dr Subhi, Assistant Dean, however, takes the easy way out by accepting the bitter reality in order to survive.

It is the protagonist, Dr Noaman, who depicts the agonies of the Iraqi intelligentsia. A reputable academic, he feels deeply humiliated when forced to give false evaluations of his students' work. He decides to retire in order to protect his conscience and moral integrity, but Dr Subhi tries to dissuade him. "You've got to stay because you're a role model scholar," he tells him. "I used to be," Dr Noaman replies, "but now I'm a bystander watching the endless falsifying of marks and results. Sometimes I take part in this process and convince myself there's no ethical issue because I'm doing it reluctantly! I'm watching everything helplessly – with my mouth shut. I can't do anything else."

Hayat, for one, could not resign herself to any of the fates pursued by the intelligentsia. Rather than putting up with humiliation and injustice, she decided to face death head on. Her suicide came as a heroic outcry against injustice.

Excerpted from a long article
and translated by Adil Babikir

HAYAT SHARARA

When the Days Grow Dark

IDHA AL-AYYAM AGHSAQAT

AN EXCERPT FROM THE NOVEL

TRANSLATED BY JONATHAN WRIGHT

I always tried to avoid rush hour on public transport, when I might have to wait a long time for the bus, so I usually left home early to be in good time for lectures, which started at half past eight. In the first half of February the cold was brittle and as sharp and dark as iron. It soon made its way through my warm clothes and reached my bones.

The sun shone in the clear blue sky with a golden glow and flooded the streets with its rays. It shone like the summer sun but it lacked the heat, as if its flame had been extinguished and it had no warmth to give the earth. I reached the main street shivering and with a slight pain in my ears: they were sensitive to the cold, as was my right eye, which started to water. I chanced upon a thin old man with a deeply furrowed brow. He had wrapped his head in a scarf and was wearing an old jacket of the kind worn by soldiers. He was squatting close to a metal drum in which he was burning tree branches and palm fronds, producing orange tongues of fire and black smoke. I stood close by and greeted him. His small eyes looked up, as hard as if the water of life had dried up in them and they had turned into pieces of cloudy glass. He returned my greeting with respect and said: "Move closer to the fire. It won't last long. It needs more wood."

I put my hands out to the fire and leaned over towards it a little as the old man continued: "If I had some tea I wouldn't feel the cold. Fire and tea together warm up my bones and cheer me up. I used to drink it all day long. That's what I love and need most."

"And why are you sitting in the street in this cold?" I asked.

"I'm waiting for them to come and take me to work cleaning the public gardens or the streets or to do any other kind of work. It makes no difference to me. I've worked as a farmer and as a soldier in the Popular Army. I fought on the Gilan-e Gharb front and I was almost captured but I miraculously survived."

"Don't you have a pension?"

"I do, but it's not enough to buy even half a kilo of tea. Before sanctions it covered all my needs, but now I go hungry if I don't work. So every day I wait at one of these places where people come looking for workers."

What he said set me thinking: I had applied for retirement two weeks previously and this academic year would be my last at college. I was worried that the prices of many things were rising so sharply that my pension would barely keep body and soul together. The plight of pensioners made me anxious, regardless of their social status. I was distressed when I once heard on the news that in Russia, after the Soviet Union collapsed and prices rose, some retired lawyers, teachers and engineers had started to beg in the streets.

I felt that they were close to me and that a common cause brought us together. We all faced the prospect of spending our old age in fear of disease and in penury, isolated from our surroundings like poor people. The world makes them feel they are outsiders and that their lives have run their course.

I hadn't applied for retirement because I was ill or unable to work. The blood still coursed in my veins, and I was eager to continue my scholarly and teaching activities. I had now reached the peak of maturity for which I had worked hard all my life. That was the dream that gave my life meaning and the success for which I had longed.

When I thought of old age I saw it as a setting sun that appears towards the end of life, with a brilliant mixture of bright and faded colours along the horizon and in the sky above. The picture it painted varied at every moment and every day, and there seemed to be no limit to the rapid changes in its appearance.

When I went for a walk at sunset and happened to see the sun, I saw myself in it. Its beauty enthralled me and my life seemed still full of warmth, splendour and radiance, just like the sun. The sun could rise every day and fill the world around me with activity and movement, as it had done in the past. It could proceed with the same bounding and ambitious strides as the young people who bustled around it. It could enter into competition with them because it was more experienced, more determined and more constant than them. I felt that I still had an advantage over them because the years I had lived gave me substance and strength — not what we see on the surface when we look at elderly people.

Things didn't change for me because of the imaginative power to which one sometimes surrenders in order to mend the cracks that have appeared in one's life or to paint life in colours that help one to continue without yielding to despair. Things changed by force of the reality that supported my talents and my work and showed me that my authority was not in decline. In fact it was growing because it was linked to the sharpness and range of my thinking and the knowledge and insight that I had, rather than to the powers of my body, which now had grey hair and wrinkles and showed signs of old age.

Retirement clearly wouldn't suit me, because it would mean turning off my active energies and moving away from an environment that was teeming with activity, young people and knowledge and from the wide and varied world in which I lived, and retreating to a narrow corner where I would become forgotten with the passage of time. Not only would I be unhappy with that: I would reject it with all the strength at my disposal.

Nonetheless I went ahead with it. I went ahead with it insistently and in the knowledge that I would not be able to change my mind. I would be disappointed and frustrated if the response to my retirement application was not positive.

So why had I done it when I rejected it so decisively? Wasn't that rather foolish and reckless? Does it not seem strange and incomprehensible? How could I reject something so strongly and yet want it just as strongly at the same time? In this story that I'm telling you I will have to answer your question and explain this contradiction that was at work inside me. But you have to bring your ear close to my lips because I have grown accustomed to speaking in a way that is alien to you – in a whisper so that no one can hear me. I have given up speaking in a normal voice because I'm haunted by fear, not just in my conscious mind but in all my senses and throughout my body. My hands tremble if I hear myself speaking loudly. My knees wobble. My eyes wander. The tip of my nose twitches. I start to hyperventilate, my saliva dries up and my blood freezes in my veins. I become the lightless shadow of a human form, a paper structure that's frail, empty and jittery.

In order to remain myself, I learned to speak in a whisper and I grew accustomed to looking around in all directions before speaking – so much so that my neck became amazingly flexible. My head could make a full circle and then turn back to where it started. I did all this to make sure that no one suspicious could hear me. I was worried about eavesdroppers, either human or mechanical, and about their sensitive antennae, which might be able to probe the inner workings of my mind and read my very thoughts, cast light on them and catch me red-handed thinking them.

Fear first appeared before my eyes like a flash of lightning that caught my attention and then disappeared. But it didn't go away completely: it reappeared from time to time in various degrees of strength and with various dimensions.

It took the form of thick grey smoke that twisted and rose in visible circles and then spread far and wide, worming its way deep into people's minds, where it left grey and gloomy traces.

No one was immune from it. People of every kind felt it – the poor but also the rich, who were usually spared the injustices, the disasters and the miseries that afflicted ordinary people.

This time the rich were also terrified and were subject to the same humiliation and hardship. With heads bowed, they kneeled and prostrated themselves to it. Different groups of people felt it in different ways. Some of them saw the fear as black bats flying chaotically and at random, smashing into people's faces. Others saw it as a strange bird with vicious wings as sharp as saws, and others as a sticky gelatinous substance that made them feel nauseous. For some people fear assumed corporeal form, when they were thrown into dark prisons, detention camps and torture chambers, or into the jaws of sudden death, or when they suddenly disappeared and their fate remained unknown. No creature could escape the fear, even those who enforced fear directly through their words or deeds. Those were more frightened that others because they lived at the heart of it day and night. Traces of it even stuck to their clothes. It was evident in the way they walked, the way they looked around them, and in their cruel glowering eyes, which radiated evil and intimidation. These were the first things one noticed in them.

If some of one's senses, such as the senses of smell, hearing and touch, could remain mute and impervious to the fear, the sense of sight always gave it away, because the eyes are a mirror that reflects what the hands are doing and reveals the terror, the anger and the scorn that lie beneath the surface. Speaking in their own silently inquisitive language, the eyes said that people were born free, as Rousseau said, and that they came into the world to live in freedom and safety, but in fact they live in fear and dread. With the passage of time people began to turn a blind eye to the fear. They grew used to living with it in order to stay alive. They instinctively clung to life and would submit to anything for its sake. They raised white flags and, in terrified whispers, told each other what had become of all those who had shown any kind of resistance to the injustice they had suffered. Defiance was forbidden and any sheep that strayed from the flock had either to meet their demise or return to the flock after being taught a harsh lesson that would continue to haunt them in all their comings and goings. After the lesson the sheep would willingly follow the path set for them, without anyone apparently forcing them to do so. Gradually and in various ways, everyone swallowed the pills of fear. They swallowed them one by one over long periods, and the pills left signs of anger and resentment on their faces. This might appear in the form of a pallid smile, an indifferent shrug of the shoulders or a supercilious look.

Everyone knew that they were totally defeated and that they had to accept this and surrender to it. If they heard that unknown people had resisted, a glimmer of joy lit up in their eyes. But it soon faded because they knew the horrific end to which defiance led. But people cannot remain themselves after they have gone through so much anxiety, deprivation and humiliation and after they have lost a dream that flaunts life and makes life beautiful.

At that point despair came to them and opened its arms to them and they put their arms around it and it led them on its way. They embarked on pleasures and forbidden sins. They no longer felt they had lost. In fact they thought they had won, as they plucked the fruits of easy money, slept with young women and drank alcohol, which took them to an imaginary world embellished with partying, women, and projects that brought in endless money. They thought they had tamed their fear and could now take advantage of it – for every cloud has a silver lining. They thought they could exploit fear for their own self-indulgent ends.

This did not happen in just any ordinary modern city, like the hundreds of other cities whose names you can find on a map of the world. It happened in an ancient city of wide renown, a city whose very name evokes a variety of ideas in the minds of listeners. It suggests glory, prosperity, a gentle and affluent lifestyle and a civilisation with roots that date back to ancient times which is even mentioned in cuneiform writings from the Babylonian and Assyrian eras.

That city is Baghdad, which has had several names since Abu Jaafar al-Mansour made it the capital of the Abbasid Empire that he founded. Arab civilisation flourished in the city and it become a beacon of light to the world in the time of his successors. Mansour called it the City of Peace because it lay on the banks of the Tigris, which was called the River of Peace because it brought fertility and bounty to the land and the people. It has been said that the name meant it was "the City of God". It has also been called the round city, because it was built to a circular design that has been imitated by many Islamic and foreign cities. They also called it al-Zawraa', allegedly because the inner gates of the city were not aligned with the outer gates. The name Baghdad is not confined to Iraq; other towns across the world have adopted the name because people loved the city of Haroun al-Rashid and wanted to immortalise its glories, which continue to perfume the present with the fragrance of that distant past.

This is the city where I stopped to warm myself on the flames of the old man's rapidly dying fire and thought about the chances of a bus coming soon. If it was late I would be out of luck because I wouldn't find anywhere to sit and I would have to stand all the way. But luck was on my side that day and the bus arrived seconds after I stopped and there were plenty of empty seats. I got on the bus with my mind at ease and found myself a seat that would save me from jostling with those standing. By the time the bus approached its destination, those standing would be squeezed up against each other like sardines in a can. But my peace of mind was soon disturbed when, half way through the journey, we ran into a traffic jam that stretched out in front of us as far as we could see.

We waited a long time and the passengers looked anxious. They were all on their way to work and had to arrive by a certain time. We all assumed there had been an accident that had obstructed the normal flow of traffic, which was piling up by the second. When I looked back a few minutes later I couldn't see the end of the tail-back.

My anxiety turned to fear when I imagined being late for my first lecture, although I would normally have arrived half an hour before it began. When going to work or visiting people I always tried to be punctual. I calculated the time with a precision envied by everyone who knew me. They saw it as one of my distinctive qualities.

Some of the passengers started to grumble to each other about the unexpected delay and the bus continued to make slow progress. It would move a few yards and then stop, and after more than half an hour we had covered the distance we would usually have covered in five minutes.

Department of Russan Language, Baghdad University

I hurried off the bus in an attempt to gain time, in the knowledge that every second counted. I rushed along, impelled by the fear inside me. In front of me loomed the figure of the Dean, who usually stood at the college gate in the morning to catch any teachers or students who were likely to be late for the first class. He wouldn't let them in unchallenged; he would delight in catching them and rebuking them, taking pleasure in lapses for which they were usually blameless. They were late because of events that were beyond their control, but he stalked them with a cheerful smile and treated their lateness as a black mark on their work record. He could put it under the microscope whenever he wanted and use it as the basis for a decision against them that would make their lives hell.

I reached the college building and before I could even see him I could hear his voice reprimanding people and asking loud and angry questions. The fear grew inside me and started to descend to my knees and feet and rise to my throat. As soon as I was near him, he put out his arm, looked at his watch and stretched his neck, leaning his head back a little. He looked at me confidently and reproachfully and spoke firmly and with authority. "Doctor Noaman, who prides himself on his punctuality, is five minutes late for his first class!" he said.

So many times I had avoided ending up in this horrible situation! To do so I had wasted half an hour or more of my valuable time every morning – denying myself the pleasures of sleeping in, having breakfast at my leisure and getting dressed slowly! Now all my efforts had gone to waste through one inauspicious encounter, and I had to justify my lateness. I smiled guiltily and my voice changed.

The words came out weak and submissive. "There was a collision between two cars and it held up the traffic," I said.

He pursed his lips with indifference. "In you go, in you go," he said disdainfully, arrogantly and quickly, as if he wanted to see the back of me. "If the students don't come to the lecture room I'll consider you absent from the first class and I'll submit a report to the university."

I headed straight to the lecture room. My heart was cowering, my eyes were troubled, my steps were heavy, my spirit was sad and everything around me cast a chill. I went into the lecture room, which was still completely empty, and took my place on the chair on the dais, which was one step up from the rest of the room. The height of the dais – the focal point for the audience – was meant to symbolise the importance, superior status and authority of the professor. I rested my head on my hands, waited for students to arrive and stared into space. I couldn't hear any footsteps. The corridor was quiet and a draught blew in through the broken windows. The students rarely attended classes in the first two weeks after the Spring break and they often came late to the first class anyway, especially in winter. If they came into class and sat down they would stare at the dais, apparently attentive, but their minds would be elsewhere – with their worries, their sorrows and their crazy ideas, while the professors went on speaking, saying what they had to say even if they didn't believe it was useful or that the students were listening. Sometimes the students would glance briefly at their watches, a sign they were bored with the lecture and were growing impatient at the passage of time. But the professors would continue as if they hadn't noticed. They didn't change the way they sat up straight in their chairs or their solemn tone of voice. Unlike the students they didn't show their boredom by looking at their watches, because that wouldn't be appropriate. They had to maintain their dignified demeanour while seated on the dais.

The Dean's scornful words – "In you go, in you go" – rang in my brain like a knell of defeat. My feelings were offended and the class was cold and deserted. But I had to be patient and wait. How patient I had been! I had endured in silence, like a statue with no feelings, listening to orders and carrying them out obediently. Fear produces obedience and obedience produces submission – cold abject submission. So I obeyed orders and stood with the assembled professors as, for example, I waited my turn to be weighed. It was an offence to put on more weight than the standard set by the government, which set benchmarks according to age and height, on the grounds that physical fitness was a sign of civilisation that must be maintained in the case of prominent public servants. Imagine how I smiled and what I thought when I suddenly discovered that I was an important person that someone respected and took an interest in! That's why I and other professors like me had to keep up our appearance. Our bodies shouldn't have excess fat on their various extremities, our stomachs should be flat, we should walk fast and be agile. Those of us in our fifties were meant to look like we were in our thirties or forties. It was a culture of orders, which were planned, communicated and had to be obeyed.

So I obeyed when I and others were asked to take part in pro-government rallies and demonstrations. I would sit in the meetings, my mind wandering, listening to the speeches, the eulogies and the criticisms of the government's enemies. I would clap when I heard others clapping at a phrase or out of respect for that glorious name that shone in the sky over Iraq and whose majesty and prestige filled the land. If that name was mentioned, it had to be accompanied by applause.

It wasn't just orders that came from other people that I obeyed. I obeyed my own orders and willingly acted on my own desires and emotions. When they took the students and faculty who were less than forty-five years old off to desert training camps in the summer vacation, when the temperatures sometimes exceeds fifty degrees Celsius, I couldn't stay at home. I went to say goodbye to them, out of solidarity with them. I was obeying my own desires, also under compulsion, when I went to the cooperative to buy food and put up with standing in the queues.

I would constantly pass by the market after work in the hope of finding food I could buy at a good price. I was in pain and I felt that my stomach needed food it was used to. The shops were full of all kinds of legumes – beans, lentils, and chickpeas – and fruits displayed in great piles, bright orange, yellow and red. The sight of them stirred the senses, the eyes gazed at them, the tongue longed to taste them and the stomach rumbled in desire for them, but the prices were so high that they were out of reach. The number of shops was constantly growing and the pedlars who sold their wares from carts or on the ground were proliferating at an unprecedented rate. People turned out to buy from them rather than from the shop-keepers because they thought they were cheaper, which made the shopkeepers use carts too to maintain their sales at previous levels.

I would walk among this plenty checking the prices to find which was cheapest. Sometimes I would buy a kilo of onions, broad beans, tomatoes or aubergines. If I couldn't find anything else I could af-ford, I would make do with some chard, celery, leaks or basil, which would add some flavour to pieces of dry bread and provide the body with some of the vitamins it needed. I would buy these scanty food-stuffs with a defeated heart. Grains of all kinds were plentiful and the land that had been famous throughout history as the Land of the Two Rivers, which bestow fertility, water and greenery on their surroundings, still carried the bounty that I could see wherever I turned my eyes. Even so, people were going hungry and the sick couldn't find medicines and children were dying of malnutrition in their thousands, in their tens of thousands, every year.

People were suffering and in pain and were imploring God to help them as they saw the world closing in on them.

Fear, disease, hunger, and penury. But nothing changed, mouths remained gagged, hearts tormented, faces resentful, but people kept going and hands continued to work.

Mona Salih, the department secretary, cleared her throat at the door. I had been looking out of the window and I turned towards her. She gave me a soft smile that suggested friendliness and respect. She came towards me and offered me a red flower with tightly curled petals.

"The staff have gone back to their rooms," she said, "because the students don't show up at the start of the second week after the Spring vacation. All the lecture rooms I've been to are empty."

I looked at the beautiful fresh flower and the reproachful voice of the Dean rang in my ears. I shrank as I replied: "The Dean has me under observation and I don't want to have any trouble with him in my last months at work in the college."

"I heard the news and I came to invite you to come to the staff room with me and have tea with the other staff."

Mona had to go around the lecture rooms ten or twenty minutes after the start of each lesson and take a list of absent students from the lecturer. That way the management could check that the lecturers were all present.

The real purpose of this procedure was to find out if the lecturers were present, not the students, who turned up whenever they wanted. Sometimes they agreed amongst themselves when they would attend. Mona had often apologised for having to carry out this administrative procedure as part of her job. It was an unpleasant task for her because she understood that it implied a suspicion that lecturers were cheating, negligent or avoiding their teaching duties. I felt the same way: I saw it as a humiliating form of spying on all of us. No doubt there were some lecturers who avoided teaching so regularly that they were known to be negligent, and yet they were still immune from reproach or serious accountability. If they were held to account it would be short-lived and sometimes even light-hearted. They knew how to cover up such shortcomings in their work through sycophancy or with the presents they brought for the administrators, whether or not there was a special occasion, and with the delicious food that they offered around during breaks in the working day.

I walked side by side with Mona and she started telling me cheer-fully some of the happy and amusing incidents that had happened in past years when she was a hard-working student who hoped to complete her higher education – the hope that drives most of those who do well in their studies and who hope to work alongside their professors and have the same status as them in the future.

We walked along together: Spring laughing and Winter grey, the bright star and the waning star. Her colourful Spring-like spirit was infectious. I smiled and started to laugh at her funny stories, which I don't remember, but I complimented her and pretended to re-member them. I enjoyed complimenting her, because to me she rep-resented that beautiful aspect that we find in nature – the dappling and blending of colours, as when yellow leaves fall amid the rich fresh green, when beautiful flowers bloom in autumn, when the sun rises yellow and bright in winter, or when cool, gentle breezes blow on summer mornings. This dappling has always been present in the lives of humans and it is this that has given people joy, dignity and beauty, as in my case now.

Mona's relationship with me was normal, as with many of the young women I taught and who graduated, but she was able to change the depressing atmosphere that surrounded me and create for me an alternative that counteracted it.

In those minutes the college was different from how it had been when the Dean met me. It was changed by the tone of Mona's friendly, kind and sympathetic voice. That was all I was conscious of now and it filled me with the warmth and softness of the gentle sex, overwhelming the dark confused corners inside me.

We reached the department and junior lecturer Zahida Omar came out of the washrooms carrying the tea tray and the cups she had washed. She stopped where she was and tilted her head sideways in a cheerful, flirtatious gesture. "Dr Noaman, I've made you a magical fragrant tea. It's the colour of dark date syrup, tastes like pomegranate juice and has the effect of borage flowers on the nerves. It's a drink that dispels daily worries and I give it free to those I like. I don't want to see you with downcast eyes. Laugh and the world laughs with you! That's a saying I always go by."

I laughed at her words, which made her sound like a fortuneteller. She took my hand and led me into her sitting room, where the staff often drank tea. Dr Subhi Abdel Karim, the head of the department, was sitting there with Dr Shawkat Salman, the department rapporteur. She put the tray on the table, offered me a comfortable chair and said cheerfully: "All the bosses are gathered in my room today. I'm so happy!"

"But the big boss is missing," Shawkat commented playfully.

She shrugged her shoulders languidly and opened her sparking black eyes wide in a gesture that suggested fear. "I take refuge with God from the evil of the accursed devil. Don't mention him or he'll appear in front of us and bring a horrible smell instead of that lovely fragrance of tea."

"The Dean's happy because he managed to catch you coming late for lectures," said Subhi, addressing himself to me. "He hates it when a professor obeys all the rules and he can't find anything to hold against him. He won't let you get away with this one."

He looked at me with his cruel green eyes, which looked like cat's eyes with their combination of vigilance and ferocity. His dark brown complexion gave him a strange appearance that automatically attracted attention and at the same time made him inexplicably repellent, though maybe this was because brown and green do not go together well on the face of a human being.

He hated the Dean's despotism and the way he interfered without

REMEMBERING HAYAT SHARARA

justification in the affairs of the students and faculty in his department. But it wasn't because he liked to see the university rules enforced, but rather because the Dean encroached on his own
authority and in the his presence he couldn't say what he thought
or behave as he wished. Like the Dean, he took an especially au-
thoritarian approach towards the people in his department, seeing
them as subordinates on whom he had a right to exert his influence.
He would order lecturers to teach subjects they didn't want to teach
or to work at times or on days when they would prefer to be free.
He would penalise them for taking sick leave because he thought
they were malingering to avoid work. Sometimes he would bawl at
them in public, because he liked his voice to boom in the department like the college bell that marked the start and end of lectures.
He would threaten, intimidate, and make those who were sitting in
their rooms cower and think twice if it ever occurred to them to
act according to their desires.

"I've been working in the college for twenty-eight years and this
is the second time I've been five minutes late for work," I replied.

"At the college council meeting," he commented proudly, "he held
us responsible for the fact that the students still haven't come to
classes. The professors supported what he said and gave some ex-
planations. But I kept silent to show him I didn't care what he said."

Zahida served us steaming hot tea with a cardamom fragrance that
filled the nostrils. Drinking it and sitting in the heat from the gas
fire made us feel relaxed and created a sense of familiarity and cosi-
ness between us, as if we were members of one family drinking tea
and talking about its concerns.

"Let's leave aside what the Dean said," replied Shawkat. "We've
had our fill of that. I want to start preparing for the cultural event
in two weeks' time, so that I don't have the hassle of training the
students to perform. It will be special this year because there are
students who are talented at acting, singing and recitation, and
they're eager to work."

"The professors ought to do a number too," joked Zahida. "Why
do they only give lectures when they could sing, tell jokes and read
poetry or excerpts from plays? Personally I'd like to join my students in their other college activities, not just spend time with them
in the classroom."

"I won't let you take part," Subhi replied sharply. "We have to maintain the students' respect for us. There are lines between us and them that we shouldn't cross. You, Zahida, you're not restrained about anything at all! You have fun with the students and tell jokes as if they're your friends. I don't like this aspect of your character."

She was visibly upset and her face turned the colour of bronze. "I feel close to them," she said in a muffled voice. "I graduated three years ago and the fourth-year students still remember that I used to walk around in the courtyard and the corridors with the students."

I supported her. "Zahida likes to have fun and joke around," I said. "It's her nature. She lightens up the dryness of teaching and relieves the stress in our kind of work. What would happen if she took part in the student activities?"

She left the room, leaving us alone, and Shawkat said: "The cultural event succeeds if everyone contributes. The students are encouraged and happy when they get to know their professors outside the framework of daily work, and when they have a friendly relationship with them in the assembly hall. We have to strengthen this friendly connection. It makes them feel the human relationship that ties them to us."

"You're in charge of cultural activities in our department," said Subhi, addressing himself to Shawkat. "There's no need to bring in the other professors. Do you want to disrupt classes and have us spend time on music and partying?"

"Why do you call it music and partying?" said Shawkat. "I work hard training the students and sometimes I stay till two o'clock in the afternoon, besides doing research in books on short plays, poetry and jokes. Writing wall newspapers and making drawings for them is also tiring work for the students who do it. All this takes time, and you think I'm having fun and amusing myself!"

"We're all negligent in this field," I commented. "If it wasn't for Shawkat, there wouldn't be any cultural activity in our department. He works hard to prepare it. I think he should be thanked formally in the name of the Dean's office when the cultural event is over, to encourage him and in appreciation of his efforts."

"Everyone works hard and does their duty," said Subhi. "There's no difference between us."

"But that's a generalisation that overlooks the differences between the professors in terms of performance. In fact everyone has special talents in one field or another."

A student came to meet Shawkat so he left the room. Subhi spoke to me in a tone tinged with anger: "You want the department to thank him officially? Do you know how often he misses lectures? He does the register of students who are present and then dismisses them from the lecture room or lets them read, while he corrects their papers or copies out one of his own research papers. He's a lazy fraud and he slips though your fingers like mercury whenever you try to pin him down. But he likes singing and acting. I don't know why he didn't go to the Academy of Fine Arts, where his talents might have flourished. He knows how to influence you, and you play into his hands. I didn't expect such a suggestion from you. If he receives any official thanks, he'll be full of himself and get even more arrogant. I'll never allow that, because everyone's equal. They do the same work and they're paid the same salary. I don't want any animosity or disputes to arise between us. Everything has to proceed quietly and stay on track."

"I think that encouraging talents in any scholarly or general cultural field would incentivise professors, rather than discourage them. Besides that's the practice in other departments. You know my position on Shawkat. I don't get on with him and sometimes I don't like the way he behaves. He has offended me personally, but that doesn't mean his activities in the department are unimportant."

"Close the subject and consider it finished. Don't try to bring it up in the department council, because I won't allow anyone to embarrass me or impose his opinion on me. I have the last word here." He sealed his decisive words by rising from his chair and walking off down the corridor, striding confidently.

I went to the room I had shared with Dr Munir Mohammad for about two months. I found him sitting at the table with a collection of books. He looked relaxed and in a good mood. I thought something must have happened to cheer him up, probably some financial reward he had received.

"You look happy. You must have had some good news," I said.

He smiled and pointed to the books on the table.

"I got hold of these books," he said. "I'm not going to take them home with me because if my wife sees them she'll throw a fit and give me a lecture about not having enough money for household stuff and wasting it on luxuries. Imagine! She sees books as secondary things that we can do without. I'll put them in the table drawer and take them one by one every two or three days."

"Maybe she's right under the present conditions. They say you have a massive library with rare old books that are usually found only in public libraries."

"It's my hobby, or you could say I have an overwhelming desire to collect books. I'm weak when it comes to books. When I see them I have to buy them, even if I have to spend the last penny in my pocket. If I can't possess them I feel frustrated and I can't sit still. If I find that a friend has a book I like I try to do an exchange. I often have more than one copy of a book because I buy extra copies to swap them for other books."

He was known to borrow books from his friends and never return them. He did the same from public libraries and paid multiple fines as a penalty for losing them.

"And if your friend doesn't agree to swap the book," I asked slyly, "then what do you do?"

"To be honest I resort to devious methods to achieve my aims. I borrow the book and I don't give it back. Or I look to see if anyone else has a copy and get it from them one way or another. Did you know I have more than a thousand books I've obtained that way over the years?"

"Do you think it's appropriate for you to behave like this, or mention it in public?"

"Being appropriate has nothing to do with it. It's a psychological and intellectual need that I have to satisfy. Some people exploit this aspect of my character too. Doctor Badri forced me to pay five times the normal price for a book I bought from him. Doctor Wajdi tried to do the same thing but I managed to catch him unawares and get it off him. Do you think their behaviour was appropriate? They were trying to take advantage of this weak point of mine and extort money from me. I believe in the proverb that says 'Only a fool lends a book. A greater fool expects it to be returned.' That's why I have a clear conscience about what I do."

"Everyone badly needs money and so they behave in this way."

"I'm no better off then they are. I spent the last penny in my pocket on these books, which were brought to me by a student who has a bookshop that sells old books. All I have left is the bus fare. Can you lend me some money and I'll pay you back in three days?

I'll soon get paid for some articles I've had published in the news-papers."

"I'll lend you some as long as you keep your promise. If you don't pay me back I'll be in trouble. I hardly have enough money to last me till payday."

"I swear on my honour that I'll keep my word. You're the only person who lends me money, so I can't betray you. Otherwise I'd have to borrow money from the students, and then they'd see me as a beggar and make fun of my qualifications and my scholarly credentials."

I gave him three hundred dinars, which was worth what three dinars had been worth before sanctions. It was just enough to cover his bus fares for three days.

"My expectations from life have declined. I no longer think about going to the north in summer. I used to go to Shaqlawa. I love the orchards full of fruit trees there and the cold water that makes me feel alive again. I can no longer have geymar for breakfast with kahi and syrup. My God! What delicious food! At the last feast my daughter asked me if we could have it for breakfast on the first day, but I couldn't afford it so I said no. She kept nagging and begging me and she had tears in her eyes. Then I shouted at her and asked her to shut up. I told her we'd have to go without food for a week if I bought all that for her and she said she was willing to go without food. Imagine! Whenever I get paid for giving extra lectures or writing articles I intend to buy some for her and for myself, but I never manage to do it because there are always more important things that have to be bought. Are you going to stay at college? The students won't be coming today, they told us, so I'll be going home."

"Mona comes to the rooms at every lesson and writes down who's present."

"Let her. The rooms are empty and it's all the same whether we're there or not. I want to drop in on *Al-Usour* newspaper and give them some articles. I have a short weekly column in the paper that brings in a little money."

He started wiping and polishing his shoes in readiness to go out. Suddenly he examined his shoes. He took off the left shoe and brought it close to his eyes. He looked worried and annoyed. "What a disaster!" he said. "The leather's started to crack and come off the sole. It won't last more than a month at the most. I'll have to get

some money together to buy a new pair. And my son wants a shirt.
What can I do? You're lucky because your kids are married now and
you're not responsible for them any more. Mine are still in secondary school. Where can I get the money? Where? I work here, and I
teach evening classes, and I write at night, and all we have for dinner
is mallow, as the popular saying goes."

"God help anyone who has children at school or university. I don't
know how they manage. My wife and I can hardly stay healthy. She's
retired but she's thinking of taking in work as a seamstress to cover
our costs."

"You can earn as much sewing a dress as we earn in a month from
lecturing."

"People who do that kind of work are doing well, but sewing isn't
suitable work for people like us. I'm against it and I cannot approve
of it. My wife a seamstress! I never imagined that such dark days
would come."

"You'll be forced to sew if you retire. You'll have to sell your house
and your car. You'd better start sewing now, as long as you have the
will and the strength."

"She wants to turn the guest room into her workshop. Then we
will receive guests in the sitting room."

"You're lucky that your wife sacrifices her comfort to help you.
A good wife saves her husband from the problems that make his
head spin. I wish my wife would suggest something like that."

"Do you know what it would mean if she started work sewing?
There would never be quiet in the house! The doorbell or the telephone could ring at any time of day or night, whenever the customers feel like it. Morning, noon and afternoon. I'm used to having
order in my life, even when the children were at home with me. I
didn't let them run riot and they had to rest and eat at set times. I
can't let strangers mess with my life when I'm at an age when I need
rest and calm. On top of that, they would look down on her doing
that kind of work. It's not work for educated people. I reject it."

"But you need the money. If you can't afford to cover your household expenses from your income you'll have to take on extra work.
If I was you I'd applaud my wife and see her work as a sign of loyalty
and concern. She's taking off your shoulders a burden that you
should be carrying, so you should sacrifice some of your comfort
in return. We're going through hard times and therefore we have

to give up our old concepts and lifestyles and be practical so that we can survive."

He stood up to leave the college. He had shown his face there and in the morning everyone had seen him in the corridors, the classroom and the staff room. It wasn't his fault that the students didn't turn up to classes, and he wasn't going to wait hours for them. The Dean or the department head couldn't consider him negligent as long as he filled in the register of absent students and signed it, and as long as he also gave the two men small gifts on special occasions, and praised and flattered them in a way that would count in his favour. He straightened his jacket and closed his fancy black Samsonite briefcase – a relic of an affluent past when professors could live a comfortable lifestyle.

I opened a book and tried to read. The Dean's voice haunted me, irritated me, confused me and made me anxious. My mind wandered and I had a vision of the Hands of Victory monument – those two giant bronze fists holding crossed swords, like a triumphal arch over a wide street that served as a parade ground. Under the swords ranks of soldiers would march to their fate: captivity, death or mutilation.

State television showed these endless ranks of soldiers arranged with geometrical precision, marching in uniform to the rhythm of martial music, rifles in their hands. They were impressive in their vigour, their beauty and their strength, which made their end – bodies strewn on the battlefield, burnt or bled to death – all the more painful and tragic. I found myself under those swords and the echoes of my footsteps, my breathing and my thoughts mingled with the sound of the marching soldiers. The image of swords appeared to me whenever I was upset or thought dark thoughts or felt overwhelmed by a fate that I could not escape.

I could no longer bear to sit in the office alone, so I closed the book, put it in my bag, locked the room and left.

This excerpt was selected and translated
from the new edition of *Idha al-Ayyam Aghsaqat*
(When the Days Grow Dark) published by Dar al-Mada. 2011
ISBN: 9782843060326

GIRGIS SHUKRY

Three Poems

TRANSLATED
BY PAUL STARKEY

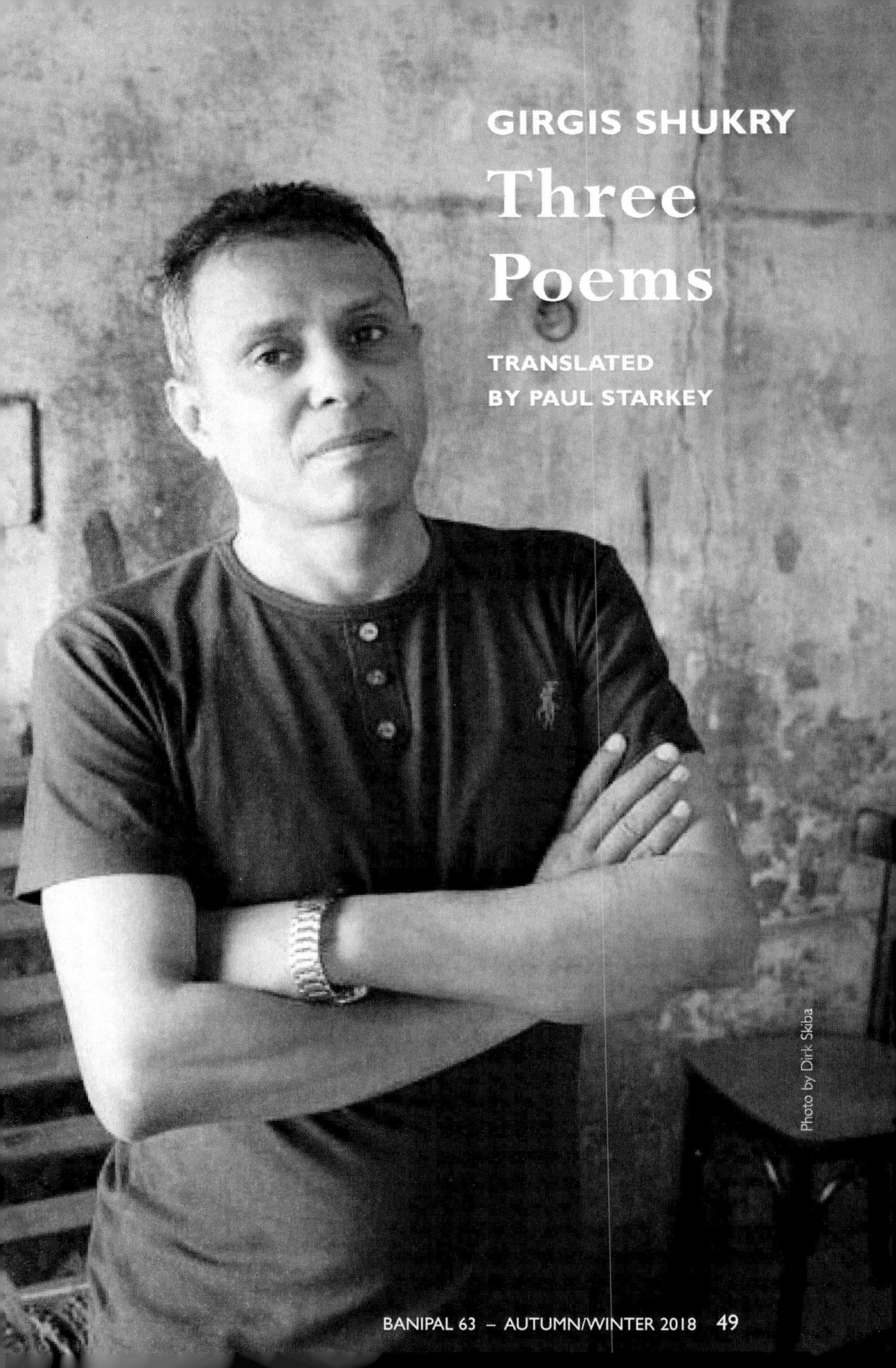

Photo by Dirk Skiba

GIRGIS SHUKRY

THE IDEAL WAY TO WRITE POETRY

1
They have mouths and ears
some are warped or second-hand,
sometimes past their expiry date.
Words spend the night in the streets,
grow sick and lie down on the sidewalks,
some are ravished
shoes trample them
they hate the nation and love music too
so they need to be washed well and prayers held
after asking them for their last wish
before they are hanged between the lines.

2
These are words,
you'll find them with the salesman and the beggar,
on the priest's tongue and the broker's,
and they stick in my mouth too.
Words don't have a knife or a stick,
the poor know them by their spirit
and I have a tale about them.

3
We have fear,
summer and winter diseases,
the whims of history,
and our master
adds to them Paradise

So who are we?
We have houses and streets,
police and a president,
and nails that grow.
We have humans and animals,
patients and thieves,
a past, and dead men writing wills.
We have women and washing lines

and words dying of laughter.
We lack nothing,
nothing do we lack.
So will you sell us a homeland, uncle,
even a used one?

4
The news arrived:
the killers are out-of-work love experts,
the madmen prophets, retired
after their jobs were abolished.

Doctors slaughtered their patients
and claimed that pain was a heresy
unbefitting a believer,

while the men of religion set up big stones,
guarded by fierce dogs, in front of places of worship
and sat, praising God and smoking,
thanking the Lord for this wisdom.

5
I dream I'm baking a state
and when it's become a really huge cake
its aroma rising
I give it to the poor.

A cake as big as a state,
tasty and enormous,
and the people dance
after eating the state
right up to its head.

THIS IS MY HEAD

1
I arrive in the world
preceded by the rites of a lady

who made noisy deals
with those who did their jobs
as mediators with the Lord
that I might arrive safely.
She fasted and prayed,
offered bread and money,
and I came confidently, with the price paid.
I owe my life to saints and jugglers.

2
Sunday is the Lord's Day
the workers' rest day, the brokers' holiday
and my birth day.

It became an eternal rest day
after the Lord decided to leave the earth
on this day,
leaving these miserable actors
to continue their roles,
content to watch from His seat
in heaven on high.

So every Sunday people started
to take off their masks and their character's clothes,
to pray humbly, without props,
for everyone to stay in their role.

3
There are things with a meaning
and things whose meaning they stole
and threw far away.

Some went to the tavern angry,
others to the market,
they bought bread and paper
and maybe knowledge.
Others took up arms.

Some went mad or died,

some are still there crying.
Was there any meaning?

4
We could not stand our childhood,
we hid it in distant stories,
we did not grow up,
while eternity grew old.

We started to cry there,
with no days in which to nurture our sorrow,

                and the light disappeared.

5
We laughed, and our tears fell by the door
The man who visited three doctors
came back with two extra eyes
and images of sickness.

He darted sharp glances
at the corners of the house
and said:
Take away the walls,
the windows no longer need questions

That day I pawned my eyes to a girl who loved the night
for a kiss and a fleeting memory.

6
My dear,
this is my hand, take it,
I have another,
I'm bored by duplication.

This is my head,
let's divide it equally
I want to be free of half the world.

I will drag my feet to another city
and teach them to ignore the road
so they cannot lead me at whim.
I will give the little creatures
to the first woman I meet.

I will live with one hand
and half a head,
with ignorant feet
and no instincts.

7
I'll put the future in the fridge
beside the tomatoes
that will be best
and throw the past down the lavatory.
I won't forget to leave the water flowing
for days and days
to stop it coming back up.
Then I'll throw a party for all my mad friends
We'll be more beautiful than this world
with our ignorant feet
and half heads
after we've demonstrated against duplication
with one hand
and donated our instincts to the girls of the road.

8
The Lord will nickname us the saints.
Perhaps He'll send golden chariots
to take us up to heaven,
with no traffic jams
to disturb the clarity of love.

Long ago a god prepared a huge feast
for our mad, murderous ancestors
and ordered his angels to carry them
on their shoulders to heaven,
eating and dancing

and keeping their love in the air.

A god was teaching the evening how to return to its brethren
when thieves disguised as kings and presidents attacked it,
slaughtered it, and made madness forbidden.

HE FOUND THE MIRROR BLANK

1
When morning is like a shabby shirt
noon a jacket with no sleeves
and night a pair of tattered shoes
I know that a graveyard is shouting,
seeking a new visitor
and that there is no time to wait.

That is what he would say.
And we were always
preparing for a funeral.

Whenever we saw someone
contemplating his clothes
our tears would flow
and one of us disappear forever.

2
He said:
This is my head.
Go there,
you'll find a chair
with Death sitting on it
and another one empty.

A musician stands between them
paying no attention,
he plays for the empty chair
and turns his back on Death.

Tell him:
My master needs some music.

3
While he lives
his feet will carry him
he doesn't know where

His hands will betray him
in handshakes with strangers
without faces.
Then he will learn sorrow.

He will live in a dream,
content to nurture time
and when he dies
no one will recall this tale.

4
He died in the market
after making a speech
which shattered the lives of those present.

After a long laugh, he cried:
Woe to you, O people!

Tears fell around his shouts.
Then they put his death up for sale
but no one came forward.

5
He carried his head to a distant land
where people do not bury their dead.
They keep them in the open air
and when it rains
each corpse lifts its umbrella
and guards its soul itself.

7

Don't believe him,
this is a man who woke late from sleep
and found, instead of his head, a hammer
that dances when he wakes
and guards his soul when he sleeps.
He wept for what was left of his limbs,
in fear, and his wailing never ceased.

9

It's not me who was here.
I don't enter my house twice
I don't wear my shirt twice
I don't see my face in the mirror
and always feel pain.

I forget the meaning,
cross out the future,
throw my shoes in the river
straight away
and teach my feet to love the earth.

10

So he started to dream
onto a big table he put
houses without people, bare trees

The earth disappeared
and his feet had nowhere to go
and there was a fire, raging, in his head.
Don't believe him,
this is a man
who woke and found the mirror blank.

Selected from the author's collection *Tuffaha la
tafham shay'an* (An Apple that Understands Nothing),
published by al-Hay'a al-Misriyya al-'Amma
lil-Kitab: Cairo, 2012

AZZA RASHAD

Prickly Jasmine

A SHORT STORY
TRANSLATED BY JONATHAN WRIGHT

Mangoes come in many varieties with many names, but generally speaking they are all beautiful and desirable and people look forward to them with longing. In our house there's more to mangoes than just that. During her first pregnancy my mother had a craving for hindi mangoes. That was in the middle of January, when the mangoes are like salty stones stuck to the branches of the trees. My father was in a quandary, but he disclosed his anxiety to a kind man who was travelling to a country the name of which my mother couldn't remember whenever she gleefully repeated the story to us. The man came back with a box of hindi mangoes and my mother is still grateful that they tasted so good. She saw the mangoes as the main reason why her baby daughter was so beautiful and, in recognition of their virtues, she chose to name her first-born Hind.

Hind, or "my mango" as Mother called her, was more beautiful and more enchanting than the models in the famous women's fashion magazines. This meant that suitors queued up at the door to marry her.

When my mother was pregnant with me, she had a craving for sardines, and she maintains that although my father was busy at the time with the annual stocktaking, he did not neglect her craving, despite the fear that I might be born with a birthmark on my face in the shape of a sardine, or that I might come out limp or with a fishy smell. To be extra sure to avoid any fishiness, they chose the name Jasmine for me. Even so, my mother likes to tease me by calling me "little sardine". But when she's angry and she says the name with her nose crinkled up, the idea of how I might have been born comes back to haunt me and I go into a corner, sniff my body and rub my face with soap again and again.

My mother puts her nose to ripe mangoes and sighs: "There are lots of them now. But they don't have any smell or taste."

But she didn't make this comment to Hisham when he brought a large box of mangoes just before the last feast. Instead she thanked him for his generosity. But when he had gone she yelled out curses on cheats and swindlers.

Mother treated Hisham kindly, which made him abandon his rustic shyness and talk and laugh as freely as if he were with family. She smiled as Hisham handed her a duck and blocks of local butter. Then she would start on hours of work in the kitchen, making us the most delicious food. When he had finished eating he would kiss her hand in gratitude, while the aromas from our little banquet rose to the nose of Umm Hamza on the upper floor, and envy drove her to detain me at the grocer's with malicious questions about when Hind was getting married. Then the fishy smell would come over me again, and I would curl up inside myself and stammer, unable to reply. That was when I was young. Now I recoil, disgusted by the smell of her sweat, which cannot be compared to the smell of the jasmine with which I now perfume my clothes. I also go out of my way to provoke her with a harassing look, quite different from the worried look in the picture that Hisham took of me when he gave me a mobile phone, after noticing I was interested in taking pictures. At the time I was thinking how long it would be before generous Hisham would reconsider his esteem for generosity. But I was so happy with the camera that I soon forgot such worries. In the next picture you can see the tips of Hisham's fingers squeezing Hind's hand as he took the plates from her. As for this charming gladiolus, I chose it from the bunches of flowers that Said brought. He was nice, romantic and infatuated with Hind, and he seemed to be offering her his heart with the flowers, while she smiled affectedly, then threw the flowers away irritably when he had gone. Mother bent down to pick up the little velvety leaves that had scattered in all directions. After a while she would shout in his face that buying flowers was a waste.

"It's no use, my dear. Once night falls, they'll be wilted by daybreak," she told him.

He stared at the flowers in embarrassment, but then he decided to stop cutting flowers for Hind to make his way to my school and then to the electricity and water companies to pay our overdue bills. But neither the flowers nor the receipts managed to change Hind's affected smile. She tossed back her long black hair, filling the air with a beguiling aroma of ripe mangoes waiting to be picked from the tree. Men stared at her and longed for her as she strode along, sleepy-eyed as though lost, looking for something without knowing what she sought, moving on, her mood swinging alarmingly – sometimes cheerful but mostly discontented. She would snarl at me and Mother over the slightest thing. Mother tolerated her with amazing magnanimity, while I ended up taking refuge with my camera, which was never out of my hands. Hind didn't like taking pictures: instead she was addicted to looking at herself in the mirror from various angles, although she looked beautiful whatever the pose. She was interested only in herself and couldn't bear to stay in the kitchen for more than five minutes. The other thing that appealed to her was listening to sentimental songs. The songs chimed with her daydreams and evoked images of the long-awaited knight she couldn't see in Hisham, who, once he abandoned his shyness, displayed a rustic nature that was incompatible with her dreams, or in Said, who was so in love with her that he gave her no space to move and irritated her, whereas I loved them both, as I love Karim now, and I hoped she would marry either of them. Mother lavished kindness on them because she was nice to everyone except when something else was required, as happened with Raouf the milkman when he changed from angel to devil, to use her words. Hind didn't like Raouf from the start. In fact she thought he was vile and, unlike Mother, she believed the stories people told about him adulterating his milk with grouting powder, formalin and other harmful substances.

Mother said that an engagement was a trial period. They all come in turn to our house full of good cheer, the evenings were pleasant, the dining table was loaded with all kinds of dishes, laughter rang out and I got used to them as if they were my relatives, until Mother turned up with an angry expression.

"A freehold apartment in her name," she would say. "Her father visited me yesterday evening and insisted on that."

At that point the dream would collapse and the result of the test would remain undecided. No one passed.

I don't know how it came about that Father would visit Mother on those occasions, whenever a suitor started to frequent the house and tried to get better terms than the examination board would allow.

Usually Hind would let one of them kiss her cheek, as if the cheek wasn't hers, and in most cases she would look away and wipe the kiss off in disgust. These things happened behind Mother's back of course, and even the one time when she was close enough to see the kiss, she didn't seem to notice. The poor woman was distracted by thoughts about her dealings with my father. Her worries were too much for her and they added a mournful tone to her voice when she told off my father: "Damn you, Abderrahim, you've had it easy and left me to deal with all this trouble by myself."

Sometimes she would lament: "A woman whose husband has died, O her suffering and need!"

She seemed weak at those moments. Her wrinkled eyelids came down over her eyes, just as when Hind treated her with disrespect and gave her orders that had to be obeyed – to cook something special for dinner or wash her clothes. Mother obeyed her orders, while I followed like her shadow. My sympathy for her made me take on some of her burdens and sometimes I felt a lump in my throat when I saw her being obsequious to Hind again in a way that was hard to justify, or when she again told me her story about the inexperienced midwife who had squeezed her first-born's soft chest as she pulled the baby out of her womb. She said this had made poor Hind "quick-tempered". As she said this, her eyelids came down more and she walked around as if with her eyes closed, unlike at other times. As soon as one of these suitors announced that he was unable to meet the financial demands of Hind's father, her eyes would widen, her voice would strengthen and she would vigorously defend our right to keep the gold the suitors had given Hind.

"It's you who broke off the engagement, so the jewellery should stay with us, since you're a man of good breeding," she would say.

"I broke off the engagement!"

Raouf was the only one who didn't turn out to be a "man of good breeding", and his voice shook the whole house: "Keep the jewellery! You bunch of gypsy crooks!"

In the end she was forced to give up the jewellery and put up with the insults from the man who adulterated milk. She wanted to put that incident behind her without us being disgraced by scandal in the neighbourhood. We had enough to handle with Umm Hazma's loose tongue and with the appearance of our apartment, where the pieces of furniture that had any value were gradually disappearing. An atmosphere of gloom prevailed until Karim knocked on the door to seek Hind's hand in marriage, and our house regained its soul. We didn't like Raouf, whereas Hisham and Said were nice: they abandoned everything and went off without further ado, and more than a year later Hisham shook me by the hand with his usual affection when I met him by chance in the street. Unfortunately the mobile phone he had given me was in my hand and he caught sight of it. I don't know what he thought, but he didn't say anything. Nor did I tell Mother how embarrassed I felt at that moment. She had already suffered enough, and when I complained to her about Umm Hamza's rudeness, her eyes popped out and she shouted: "We don't owe anyone anything!", adding that no one had helped us in hard times.

I never asked her how much she got for the gold she had sold. She didn't remember she had sold it anyway.

One wall of the balcony is covered with strings of garlic and onions, and on the floor on the other side, there's a rattan chair where a tall brown man used to sit. He had a long face and light brown eyes and he used to cut lengths of flannel cotton cloth for people, adding a few centimetres with a cheerful smile. He was kind and generous and his name was Abderrahim. Most nights he made sure to sit me on his lap and tell me stories about Tom Thumb and Ali Baba and the Forty Thieves. I didn't take in all his stories but the joy his affection brought me made me howl with laughter. Now our laughter sounds strange and hollow, and in the still of night I restrain myself, anxious not to make any movement, while I silently watch Hind toss and turn in bed. I listen to Mother's quiet footsteps in the sitting room and I feel we are players in a game, each of us pretending that everything is as it should be, as if someone has promised us that if we do this everything really will be as it should be. But it isn't Mother's fault my father died and all he left was his stake in the cloth shop that my uncle then took over. On the first day of every month my uncle gives us a tiny amount of money, with the excuse that business is bad, while we hear from other people that he makes large profits and wastes the money on his whims. Meanwhile he claims to his wife, who he is "dead" scared of and treats with kid gloves, that he is killing himself at work. It wasn't Mother's fault: she had done everything she could for us. That's why I hated Raouf, who insulted her, made a public spectacle of us and was responsible for Umm Hamza's malicious gloating. Thanks to divine justice, he met his just deserts when the police came and closed down his shop. Umm Hamza, too, shouldn't have spread her lies chatting with the grocer or loitering on the stairway eavesdropping on her neighbours. If she had stayed at home minding her own business, she wouldn't have slipped on that banana skin and broken her leg. If only she had kept her mouth shut!

Although Hind is only four years older than me, Mother thinks I am still the little girl that hid in the folds of the curtain or under the table. She thinks I don't understand the secrets she shares with Hind, so she stops talking when I appear or tries to send me off hurriedly on some pretext. This used to make me angry but I refrained from shouting: "I'm here! I may not be as useless as you think I am." I no longer get angry; now I laugh at her because she doesn't know any of her little sardine's secrets. I would probably have stayed young, a tasty morsel in fact, if it wasn't for secondary school and the stories the girls tell, which have given me experience that some people go their whole lives not knowing, as well as other skills, the most interesting of which is the art of self-defence and the most frivolous of which is the art of embellishing simple things with simple tools and a little thought. I am now so skilled at this that it no longer takes me more than five minutes in the stairwell. After that I go out into the world looking very beautiful and I no longer feel humiliated in the presence of colleagues who flaunt their beauty, which used to happen last year. Now I have a status I have earned by my own hard work. The unfortunate thing is that I'm alone. There's something inside me that makes me prefer to keep my distance and hide behind the camera, which is now my fiercest friend.

I spend the day roaming the corridors and taking pictures. I've documented girls and teachers in some funny or wild poses – things no sane person would believe. I haven't shown them to anyone. I'm happy just to have them in my possession, which makes me feel proud and sometimes safe.

More than half the pictures are of my mother – her neck drooping limp as she sleeps, her thin fingers so skilled at cutting up vegetables, her thin lips whispering "And from the evil of the envious when they envy" as she combs her long hair, most of which has turned grey, her arms swinging the censer before Friday prayers, the little tears rolling down the wrinkled skin under her eyes when she raises her voice and curses those who have wronged us, her weak laugh when she talks about my father, and her biting her lips. Beautiful shots that are spoiled only when Hind butted in and made my hand shake and the picture turned out blurred and Hind's face appeared, intruding from one side in a way that amused me but annoyed her. But she made up for it with a calm solo picture of her with a sprig of jasmine that lit up her face and her hair and made her look daintier than a crowned queen who gives commands and is obeyed. Once I asked her to take a picture of me, but she couldn't do it, whereas I've managed to take pictures of myself in poses that make me look very beautiful, pictures that have won the admiration of my colleagues and established me in their eyes as a true artist. My favourite picture is the one that shows the intelligence of a little sardine that manages to slip through a group of large dolphins that are on the attack. I took it on a school trip to the Alexandria Aquarium Museum. The philosophy teacher liked the picture but after I brought out the other pictures her face went pale. She gave a forced smile as she praised my skill. Then she blinked twice, sighed and warned me of the consequences of not understanding the ethical objectives of art. This woman doesn't know how much I like her or how much I would hate to be like her. Her colleagues burden her with extra classes and more tasks than she can handle, and she doesn't object. She hears them making jokes about how kind and stupid she is and she smiles and pretends to be deaf, and then she looks down so that no one can see her crying over "lost values". Or else she comes to give me a lecture simply because she caught me holding a tube of lipstick and giving one of my colleagues a lesson in the secrets of make-up. I don't want to be like my mother, either, despite my pathetic love for her, which makes me give in when she insists on treating me as a child and makes me accept that she allows Hind to do many things she prevents me from doing. Even the only time she saw me wearing make-up was in spite of me – I had closed the door of my room so that she wouldn't notice me, and I couldn't help listening to them bickering noisily about Karim.

"Okay, my dear, marry him. We can live with it," Mother said.

"No, I won't leave you. But we'll have to give the jewellery back to him. Don't belittle me in front of him more than you have already," replied Hind.

The plaintive love song began. Mother didn't want to admit that Hind really loved Karim. But he was the only one whose kisses mattered to her, the only one who I felt, from the first moment he came into our house, could meet her heart's expectations. I hoped she would marry him and give us some peace. All we had to do was draw his attention to the dreamy aspects of her character that were hidden behind her damned pride, but as soon as Karim asked to speed up the wedding Mother wrapped her head in a dark scarf and started complaining she had shivers up her spine. In the meantime I lived through a swirl of emotions – firstly the desire to take revenge on this conceited woman, then the envy that swept over me when I watched them exchanging long, wet and amazingly passionate kisses, and finally pity for the pretty round face that shrivelled up and turned dark like a stale loaf of bread. Despite her suffering she was less insolent towards Mother, though this didn't seem to be a good omen. The hellish looks that she started throwing at Mother presaged the imminent explosion of a beautiful ripe mango. She showed no common sense and fell flat on her face, unnerving Mother, who closed the door of her room and went for a long sleep. When she woke up she dictated my father's usual terms to Karim: "He's just like the others," she said.

"No, he's not like the others. You're the one whose eyes God has blinded," Hind replied angrily.

I know Mother often closes her eyes, but she isn't blind. She did age suddenly, however. She lost her usual vitality and her enthusiasm for making delicious meals. She became absent-minded and cut her fingers when she was cutting vegetables. I also saw her blocking her ears in pain at the babbling of the pesky woman who has been living in the basement for years. We had grown so used to her noise it was like the sound track to the film of our lives. One day I was so annoyed that Hind was constantly humiliating Mother that I stormed out of my room and screamed in anger: "Let her marry him and give us a break. I'm with you, don't worry."

She stared at me in alarm, at the shiny clips in my hair and then the varnish on my toenails. Unfortunately, I had overdone it to distract myself from them.

Then Mother shouted: "What's that shit that you've done to yourself! Go and wash your face."

On my tongue I could still taste the jasmine perfume, mixed with the taste of eye shadow powder and rouge, which the tap water washed away instantly. In the meantime I pricked up my ears to catch what Mother said as she swallowed her humiliation and kept imploring Hind.

I often get angry with my mother and I can flare up at her. I might threaten her in my imagination but I never forgive people who mistreat her and, thank God, all of them have got their just deserts without her knowing anything about it. There was that banana I ate with relish and then the skin I threw out of the front door. Then there were the complaints that the commercial fraud department and the consumer protection associations received, by mail and by telephone. After that the police turned up and shut Raouf's shop down and he had to pay several times the cost of the bridal jewellery in fees to an experienced lawyer to have the case safely dismissed. My uncle will come over to our house and give my mother our dues in full, and I'll share her surprise and joy. I won't say anything about that time when I caught sight of my uncle at the back of the shop, kneeling on top of the poor young woman who works there. It was just by chance that at that moment some little sardine went and asked him for a small amount of money, if only as a loan. That's what Mother had asked her to do and she arrived at just that moment to see what she saw. Her morals didn't allow her to tell her aunt about the man's disgraceful conduct, but the upside was that since then he's been giving my mother her full share of the money from the shop.

In the coming days we're going to arrange, as well as we can, Hind's wedding procession to her new husband's house. By the time we get home, Mother and I, the jasmine season will be just round the corner.

From the author's collection *Banat Ahlami*, published by Akhbar El Yom, Cairo 2013

Mekkawi Said 1956–2017

MEKKAWI SAID

The enchantment of Reem

AN EXCERPT FROM THE NOVEL *TO BE LOVED BY JIHAN*
TRANSLATED BY AHMED SALAH ELDEIN
WITH THANKS TO HANNAH SOMERVILLE

At the time I got to know Reem she had just lost two lovers, one after the other. She considered me no bad omen, but on the contrary drew closer to me; maybe I was a substitute for them. I saw her once, twice, five times, even, but never tried to bring myself into contact with her despite my overwhelming fascination. I revered her and took care not to be caught sneaking peeks at her; she had a ferocious side barely concealed behind her charming complexion. I remember the first time I saw her. I was sitting alone in the Odeon Hotel, downtown. I used to go there every so often to get near the writers and movie people who frequented the place, and observe their noise, their play and tussles, because of my nostalgia for the times when my uncle Hossam took me to their haunts. He considered himself one of them, or perhaps a fan. He introduced me to the place in the latter part of his life. We used to share drinks and talk, and it was because of him that the place became one of my beloved spots.

Sometimes, I went with Emad. He used to disturb me with his attempts to introduce himself as a lyrical poet to celebrities if any were present, trying to market his naïve songs. I blocked him more than once, so he hated the place and started to drive me to other entertainment hot spots full of whores who knew him well and so provided the best services for the lowest prices.

Enchanted by Reem, the frequency of my visits increased so as perhaps to see her, but she made only rare appearances. She came a few times by herself, and once in the company of her friend Stella, whose name I got to know later. Sometimes she was surrounded by a group of highbrows belonging to the cinema and theatre industries – directors, writers, producers and cinematographers – assailing her ears with their talk, while she bobbed her head and smiled. I never caught her speaking, just being an attentive listener. She was white and pink-pigmented, slender, while her black hair was mid-length. Her face was captivating with the Asmahanian beauty spot on the side of her mouth. She wore a platinum bracelet around her leg like an anklet.

Usually she joined the gatherings of highbrows. Some of them were no strangers to me. I talked to them about my uncle Hossam who had loved writing colloquial poetry. But I dared not approach her while she was in their company as I feared rejection and thus losing her forever. When I came with Emad to have a close look at her, which had never happened with the woman of my choice, Jihan, he tried to push me to introduce myself to her by any means, and kept rebuking me for not taking a step forward, accusing me of being a coward. At this moment she had been about to leave after paying her bill. To my surprise, Emad took his keys and golden cross from the table, whispering to me to catch up with him and talk to her in the elevator. He had kept nagging me about this until I reproached him, hard. After that I spied on her via some acquaintances. Each identified her differently. One said she was a theatre actress who had stayed for a while in Europe to study, then come back to pursue her artistic career. Another said she was getting ready to pass her placement tests to work as an announcer on TV. I was not able to avoid her, which would have to let my desire wane, especially after my unsuccessful efforts to get closer to Jihan. Reem was the ultimate antidote.

My personal miracle happened when she entered the hotel lobby. The feminine voice knocked me down with a feather. She was walking out of the hotel manager's office, hurling abuse, while the receptionists were in a state of panic, gazing fearfully at the manager's door. Every time the security supervisor tried to shut the door, the lady's voice became louder, ordering him to leave it open. She tried to attract the attention of the guests so they might listen to the absurdities taking place in the hotel. Driven by curiosity, I moved with others from the elevator towards the room. She was standing in front of the door, calling on guests to follow her in angry and hysterical tones. Her face was flushed pink. Up to that moment, I didn't realize that it was her . . . Reem. I was terribly confused as it was the first time she had seemed to speak to me directly, eye to eye. However, I was but one face in the crowd. Unusual for me, I seized the opportunity. I broke out into the room and listened to the problem: she had been about to stop a cab in front of the hotel when some street sellers — who sell services to tourists, at a material or moral cost — approached her, and she had ignored them. Her indifference provoked them, and they harassed her insolently, thinking she was a foreign tourist rejecting their company. None of the passers-by had intervened and thus their agitation heightened. A cab stopped and she quickly threw herself into it and called them names from the window. A daredevil among them recklessly stopped the cab; another one pulled her out of the cab and slapped her viciously, and a third snatched a platinum bracelet from her ankle. Then they threw her back into the cab and vanished. She went to Abdeen police station, where they showed her photos of a few suspects and issued a report. But she sensed insincerity in their approach and regretted that she hadn't taken revenge with her own hands, or with her father's gun if she had had it in her bag. She told us she had returned to look for them and to rebuke the hotel's security officers, who had been watching from behind the glass doors of the entrance without offering a hand, even though they recognized her as one of the hotel's regular guests. A security guard objected, swearing they hadn't seen anything, and the hotel manager supported him. She snapped, and insulted the manager with an abhorrent word that scared the hell out of me. To stop things deteriorating further, I asked her to come with me and said I would deal with it. She suddenly looked me in the face, appraising me in shock as if I were a creature from outer space, just landed in the middle of the room. She said disparagingly: ""Who are you? Who gave you the right to interfere?" Afraid of losing momentum, I immediately answered that I was one of the hotel's clients, and mentioned the names of some of those she mixed with. She stared at me for a few seconds and then asked about my job and how I would help her. I told her firmly to follow me, understanding that that was the right way to deal with her. I realised that from the sound of her steps behind me, from her sitting still in the cab I called, and from her showing no reluctance when I changed its direction to Giza Security Directorate, where Emad had been transferred not long before this incident. Emad received us in his office with exaggerated delight, feigned awe, and gave me sly glances, as if to say: "You bastard! You hooked up with her and come up here to my office!" And because that wasn't true, I was offended by his behaviour. The outrage in my voice was clear when I demanded he sit and listen to us. I introduced her to him by name, which surprised her, so I told her I knew it from the argument with the hotel manager. Emad listened to her story quietly, then picked up the phone, telling them he was leaving the office. He asked Reem to finish her drink quickly as he took his gun from the desk drawer in an arrogant and showy manner that incensed me but I reluctantly kept quiet. Then he put back the gun into his bag and donned his non-military casual jacket that was hanging on the chair in front of him. He dismissed his military driver and drove the car himself, saying he would take us to Abdeen police station. Reem sat in the back and I paid her no attention, cringing with worry over what Emad might do. He was aware that I liked her and would certainly do whatever possible to make her happy. But I was afraid that his excessive flamboyance might uncover my attachment to her. Climbing up the stairs to the commissioner's office, I implored him to tone it down. He smiled at me without comment. In the commissioner's office, Emad outdid himself and the commissioner was frightened out of his wits. In a matter of half an hour the men who had attacked Reem, whom police officers had earlier claimed were unregistered and therefore difficult to trace, were right there in front of us. The commissioner yielded to Emad's superiority and presented the men, unshackled, for him to deal with, while he left the room. Emad exploded violently, lashing out with kicks and blows from his gun to their bodies. They screamed and begged Reem for mercy but she stood there smiling contentedly, contemplating the flowing streaks of blood. She asked Emad to stop and he did so immediately. She told him to make them stand in a line in front of her. He did as she asked, while trying to prevent them from collapsing to the floor. Like a professional ballerina, she bent down, took off a shoe, and started slapping their faces, their heads and whatever parts of their bodies she could reach. She sighed with satisfaction and told them to keep her bracelet as a souvenir. She thanked Emad and looked at me for what seemed a long time, seeing me as her saviour.

Out in the street Emad offered to drive her home, but she turned him down with a smile and said she was going to call on some friends. Foolishly, Emad told her we were going to a party, and he was about to invite her to join us when I abruptly cut him short and told him to get in the car. Leaving her behind, Emad eyed me with a bewildered look on his face and said: "Did you ever learn anything from me? The girl was totally in your hands and you let her go that easily!" I asked him to drive us to a place where we could enjoy ourselves and to stop giving naïve advice. As he drove, he asked: "Did she take your phone number?" I replied: "No." The steering wheel shuddered in his hands and he muttered: "I'll eat my hat if she ever pays attention to you again."

I vanished from the Odeon Hotel for more than two weeks and instinctively felt that she would look for me but would find no trace of me as none of my close friends there would give her my phone number. Going directly to Emad in the Department to ask about me was not an option either, as I imagined that that would hurt her pride and prestige. As a matter of fact, though I had yearned to be her friend for many months, now, after offering her help, I had no more longing for a relationship based on gratitude so I avoided all the places where she might catch sight of me. However, she found me through a hotel client who had sought my supervision on the interior decoration of his house. I had protested to him that I worked only on concrete constructions, but he had my business card. Via this card Reem contacted the company's headquarters in Giza and came to see me. She asked me why was I avoiding her. I answered with excuses and arguments that she did not accept. She demanded I join her for dinner and I agreed immediately. We went to the nearest restaurant where I talked about my work and the reason I mingled with highbrow people and artists. I spoke about my uncle and the ambitions that destroyed him. She told me about her studies at the Faculty of Arts, then at the Institute of Dramatic Arts, and about some of her travels to the Gulf and Europe. Before entering the restaurant I had stipulated that the dinner would be on me and she had agreed. When the conversation faltered, she nodded at me to ask for the bill. After I had paid, she said with a smile: "Are you satisfied now? Next time it's on me." I objected that I would never accept that since I had done nothing to deserve it. She laughed uproariously, saying: "You are so old-fashioned . . .You think I invited you out of gratitude, even though I have already thanked you and meant it sincerely." Then she added coquettishly: "It seems you're going to tire me out. Well, carry on to your heart's content." We exchanged phone numbers. As she left, I phoned Emad; I was on cloud nine, and asked him to meet me in one of the bars on Al-Haram Street where we used to meet and have fun. He asked hastily: "Put me at ease. Did she fall head over heels for you?" The words upset me so I didn't answer.

At her request we met several times afterwards. I realised she was a sort of culture vulture and I was slightly panic-stricken by the deluge of readings and information that kept whooshing through my ears, particularly when she told me she read in two languages as well as Arabic. I detested this highbrow showing-off, and I thought I would soon be breaking off our relationship. When she stayed away from me for a month I paid no attention until one day I received a phone call from her. She started by poking fun at my indifference. Then she told me about her trip to Europe, and that the data roaming on her mobile phone was turned on so as to receive calls from Egypt. She reproached me sharply, and hung up. I was bothered by her behaviour, but cheered up a little as I realised I had her under my spell; I had made my presence felt close to her heart. The next day I phoned to invite her to go out, and she pretended she was busy, as I had anticipated, and asked to postpone it for a few days. Eventually we met up. We stayed out so long and had so many drinks that we were completely intoxicated. She seemed to be quite incapable and I was afraid to let her go home in such a state. I suggested dropping her off at her house and she said nothing. Inside the cab, she muttered the address. Halfway there, the driver was about to make a wrong turn but she redirected him, with vacant eyes and mouth wide open. Then she buried her face into my chest and mumbled about needing to vomit. I was about to tell the driver to stop, but her hand stopped my mouth, asking me falteringly to let him proceed as the house was nearby. She was right; within ten minutes we were inside. She told me to make myself at home while she went to the bathroom. When she returned, she was a wet nymph, no traces of alcohol discernible on her face or in the way she walked.

Seeing I was baffled, she sat down face to face, explaining confidently that taking a shower made her sober up. Besides, she said, the driver's open window had hit her face with cold air that had mitigated the effect of the alcohol. I believed her then, but as we got to know each other well, I realized that she had an innate talent for acting.

Combing her long black hair, she started to chat, asking me if I had a pair of sunglasses. Before I could express my boggle-eyed astonishment at asking for sunglasses in the middle of the night, she moved towards her bag that lay right beside me, took out her own glasses, got me to put them on, and then sat close to me. She came very near, peering into the lenses, tidying and stroking her hair and smoothing it back. She seemed very pleased with how she looked as she took the glasses off me and said with a smile: "Merci." I shrank back, annoyed that she had made me her mirror-holder. It seemed she realised the same thing as she let out a burst of laughter, saying: "What's wrong with you?! Are you scared, sitting there not moving a muscle? Don't you worry! I'm not going to rape you." I was taken aback by her boldness as she became even more provocative, wryly commenting: "I will let you submit to me without resisting."

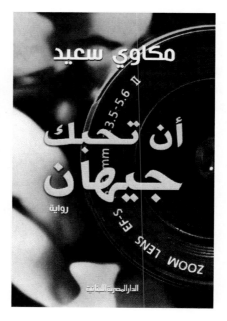

Excerpted from
Mekkawi Said's novel
An Tahibbaka Jihan
(To Be Loved by Jihan),
Published by al-Dar al-Missriya
al-Lubnaniya,
Cairo 2015

AHMED SALAH ELDEIN

Mekkawi Said's last novel

The late Mekkawi Said's novel *To Be Loved by Jihan* (*an tahib-baka Jihan*), was a sweeping success in Egypt when it came out in 2015. The author again tackled serious issues in a pseudo-realistic manner. Reading it, you immediately sink into a state of déjà vu, as though you had experienced the same in your own life, or had seen the events happen to people you know. Herein lies the novel's trick. The neutral and melancholic atmosphere removes the reader by a degree from the characters' tensions and prevents us from taking sides. The reader is left to decide for themselves how to view the novel. Multiple interpretations are possible.

Structurally, the polyphonic *To Be Loved by Jihan* focuses on the personal dilemmas of its characters, with each voice telling its own story. These stories are interwoven to draw a larger portrait. It's as if every character blogs their own details and hands the pen to the next. The novel's focus and forward motion varies so that it that reflects the inner realities of characters and their circumstances.

Emad, for instance, is seen from within. Although his outlook and behaviour feel typical of an Egyptian police officer, he still evokes sympathy as we learn the reasons he became the person he is. Tamim is a talented sculptor who has a dream of being a great artist, but fails. The two Egyptian communists, Ahmed's uncle and his neighbour, emerge faintly in the novel, as apparitions of a dream that passed away. Nobody wins, as the novel is devoid of black-and-white morality and personal victories.

It is Ahmed Eldawi who is at the centre of *To Be Loved by Jihan*. As an anti-hero, Ahmed regards life negatively, neutrally and coldly. He is an architect who lost his faith in art and himself after the 1992 earthquake, which sparked a crisis on both personal and professional levels. This may explain the novel's loose and fragile structure, parallel to the loose and fragile buildings destroyed by the quake. Indeed, Said seemed to intentionally gather this band of defeated antihero characters as his novel's building blocks to convey the status quo of a country in crisis. The Egyptian revolution gathered the scattered pieces of defeated human souls. It was akin to an endeavour towards healing, another earthquake: but this time human, intentional, and a cry for social justice, bread, and freedom.

None of the characters in the novel was involved in the events of the revolution except Ahmed, and his involvement was slight. Even after this man-made "earthquake", the country remains autocratic and justice seems impossible, the middle class astray. Indeed, the Egyptian middle class almost disappears amid wild new realities, lost in their everyday problems and their own lives, a place where even love is far-fetched. They seem to be a relic of a past when the middle class was a robust building block in society.

Said's core female characters court controversy. There is Jihan, the ethically determined and arrogant coquette, and Reem, rebellious and emancipated. Ahmed loves Jihan with a kind of love that seems unfulfilled and impossible, while his relationship with Reem functions as an antidote to the pains and frustrations he experiences with Jihan. Jalila, his wife, exerts every effort to help Ahmed and make him happy, and she is eventually deserted. His mother is the strongest among them, an Upper Egyptian woman who cares more about her brother than her son. She also has the upper hand in her relationship with her husband. Together with Caroline, Emad's beloved, they project a slightly more positive image of women than the rest.

The sudden death of the excellent Mekkawi Said on 2 December 2017 was a shock for his friends and readers. His place in downtown Cairo had become, over 20 years, a salon where people would gather around and talk about different issues. You could meet this award-winning Egyptian novelist, short story writer, and essayist any time, by just dropping in and approaching him, the modest, down-to-earth man that he was, as he sat in a corner of al-Bustan Café. You would always be welcome. The man of letters who talked with everyone, and gave a hand to whoever needed help. He is hugely missed.

Fishermen
Oil on wood
150x100 cm
Alexandria 1956

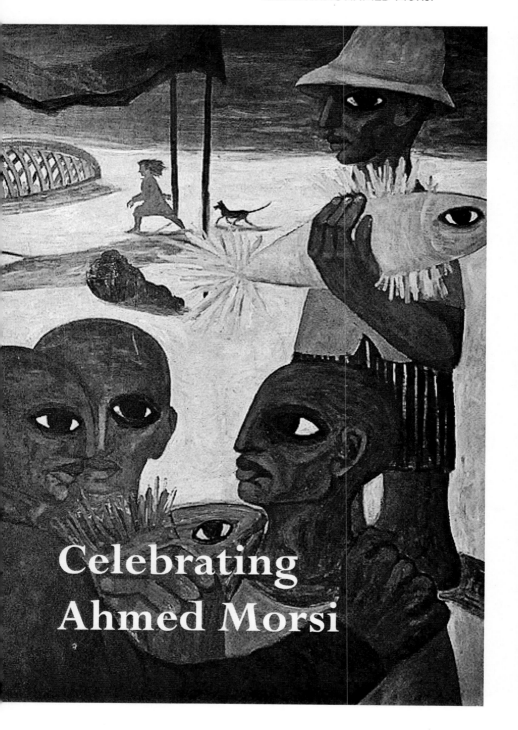

Celebrating
Ahmed Morsi

Ahmed Morsi in his home in Manhattan in 2007, Photo by Samuel Shimon

A hmed Morsi was born in Alexandria, Egypt in 1930 and grew up there. After graduating in English Literature, and publishing his first poetry collection at the age of 19, he went to study art in the Alexandria studio of Silvio Becchi. From early on, he became a part of Alexandria's literary and artistic society and by his early twenties was showing his works in group ex-

hibitions with Egypt's most notable modern artists, including A Al Gazzar, H El Telmisani, I Massouda, F Kamel, H Nada and M Moussa. He was one of the few handpicked artist selected to exhibit at the opening of the city's Museum of Fine Arts.

Amhed Morsi lived for two years in Baghdad, from 1955 to 1957, which was a time when Iraq was experiencing a cultural renaissance and Baghdad was a literary, artistic and intellectual hub. There he developed lifelong friendships and working creative relationships with Iraqi writers and painters, among them Abdel Wahab Al Bayati, Fuad Al Takarli and Ardash Kakavian. He was also able to nurture his talent for art criticism and wrote on major Baghdadi exhibitions for local newspapers.

Back in Egypt, he lived in Cairo, working alongside acclaimed playwrights Alfred Farag and Abdel Rahman Al Sharkawi, designing stage sets and costumes for The National Theatre and the original, Khedieval, Cairo Opera House. In 1968, he co-founded the avant-garde magazine *Gallery 68* with Egyptian authors Edwar Al Kharrat, Ibrahim Mansour, Gamil Atteya, Sayed Hegab and others, and served as its Editor-in-Chief. *Gallery 68* became the voice of the new modernism and Ahmed Morsi began to publish a number of critical articles on both art and literature. In his 1995 show, he pioneered a new creative vehicle, "The Artist's Book", that led to a new biennial exhibition, The Artist's Book, being established in Alexandria, under the auspices of the Biblioteca Alexandrina.

In 1974, Ahmed Morsi moved to New York City, where he continues to paint and write. In 1976, like many other artists in NYC, he took up printmaking, adding yet another string to his creative bow, and in the last 20 years embraced photography.

ALFONSO ARMADA

The door to the beach of time

Although Ahmed Morsi has been living in New York for decades, he has never fully abandoned his past life. That is, his native city. If Alexandria exists, it breathes in his memory. But he does not paint what once was; he paints a spirit, an atmosphere extinguished in the geopolitical and moral seas of nowadays, a century that breaks its knuckles against us. Mural paintings, purity, silence. Horse heads, stone heads, asexual bodies, absence of time, eternal time, time that returns like the sea against the beach of time of Ahmed Morsi. Poetry finds a clear and mysterious road towards the crystallization of painting and vice versa: paintings find their way towards the mind of the painter through the poetry with which he contemplates the world and his dubious shadow upon it.

Painting is a figuration of the soul, while poetry moves into the field of resonance of the human voice, which is the one that translates thought or at least attempts to do it: because reason is made of quicksand. That is why in Ahmed's paintings we read images of words that recall a forming thought that cannot and will not be told except in this way, without words, with a terrifying, familiar silence. As if he had linked, via a secret internal passage, the secret chamber of the Pharaoh's servants with the tombs of Juan Rulfo's ancestors and his "Pedro Paramo". Had I not known Ahmed Morsi to be a poet, I could have succumbed to the relatively easy temptation of saying that he paints poems. But that would be lapsing into a degradation of both registers, which are here related to one another like the left and right sides of the brain: without words, with its body

(Nostalgia Series), Fisherman & maroon bird with grey sea. Etching & aquatint on zinc plates, 1976

turned into a sort of delta and a sort of hinge where voices, full of images and emotions, lie down next to images locked into the paint- ings, which themselves unleash emotions hard for us to translate into sentences. They appeal to a territory that, though populated by reminiscences directed to and located in Egypt, in Alexandria, under the sand, in the hieroglyphics, in hieratism, in the silent profiles of figures who sew, or knit, or paint, or write, allows them to retell at the same time the beginning of sight, of their way of seeing when heat makes the horizon reverberate and the clarity of things remains self-said.

* * *

When I read the poems of Ahmed Morsi I begin to travel. I am not going to say he was waiting for me in New York because I did not know I would be coming to spend some of the crucial years of my life here, nor that he would be waiting at the other side of a steel table at the United Nations, while delegates' voices speak to an auditorium of mirrors in the great rooms of the General Assembly and the Security Council. But the truth is that almost from the first moment, we speak through a third language that we share but which is not our own, is not the one we speak in our dreams nor the one we speak when we try to describe the way the first beach was, the metallic locks of the old shops that sold chandlery and rigging, dates and corn, fish flour and herring, coffee, couscous, codfish, spices, reels, feathers, ink and reams of paper, brushes and linseed oil, copper wire, wax, matches, chickpeas, books and newspapers, soap, cork, cane, esparto, oil lamps, pins and nails, paints, knives, and paintbrushes and aqua fortis and potatoes, almonds and candy, pasta, glue, dictionaries and shoes. We do not need many words to understand one another.

* * *

His world seems airtight, impenetrable, protected by a lattice of silence and loneliness. It is there, however, in all its intensity, in its lack of emphasis, in its frankness. He does not highlight, does not scream, does not point. He half opens the door that leads to the beach of time and invites everyone who wants to enter it, those who dare to read, leaving behind the noise, the voices, and the echoes of those who are fabricating the world with blows of an axe. And they forget that we are going to die, that in the face of all that vibrant future there are men like Ahmed Morsi who know how to pronounce silent syllables, stakes sunk in the sand, horses that observe us, eyes that are our own, heads that we rock in our arms so that all is not extinguished when we close our eyes and the sea comes to beat with its grey ink upon this strange place called existence.

Translated from the Spanish by Sara Murado
© Gypsum Gallery, Cairo

Self Portrait
Acrylic on canvas
231cm x 154cm
Cairo 2006

SALAH AWAD

Ahmed Morsi:

The Poet

From the outset, quietly and relentlessly, Ahmed Morsi sought to depart from conventional ways of writing poetry, painting, and engraving on zinc plates. He sought to see the objects around him with the eye of the primitive artist, who is not occupied with decoding but rather intimately connecting with the surroundings, making them his incantation against unforeseen harm.

Poetry, taken as the earliest endeavour to unearth what is fresh and vulnerable in the universe, was the prime source of inspiration in Morsi's life. Morsi is a contemporary of two great poets – Salah Abdel Sabour and Ahmed Hijazi. Before he was twenty years old, Morsi had published his first poetry collection. He continued to write well into the late 1960s, when he abruptly shifted to painting, and went through many stylistic phases while always remaining on the verge of experimentation. What set Morsi apart from his counterparts was his proximity to French poetry and surrealism; he would somehow remind the reader of some leading figures of surrealist poetry.

He moved to Baghdad in the mid-1950s and worked as an English language teacher. It was there at a café called Brazilian that Morsi by chance ran into the famous poet Abd al-Wahhab Al-Bayati, and two other writers, Abdel Malik Nouri and Fuad al-Takarli. He had the opportunity of studying modern Iraqi poetry, which began with Badr Shakir al-Sayyab, Nazik Al-Malaika, Abd al-Wahhab Al-Bayati, and Buland al-Haidari. The influence of al-Sayyab and al-Bayati on Morsi's poetry is clear, especially in the poems written during this episode of his life up until the late 1960s.

As a poet and artist, Morsi contributed to *Gallery 68*, an avant-garde magazine that played a crucial role in highlighting the most prominent Egyptian prose writers of the 1960s (short story and novel). Morsi's poetry was never hindered by his other artistic occupations, including his work for the aforementioned magazine. His poetry offered an intriguing literal rendering of his paintings, while also feeding on the elements of fine art. Morsi's poetic image is innovative but doesn't lack specific reference, despite his commitment to the traditional form. He sought to create paintings inside the poem where the rhythm is set by invisible brush strokes, creating a sense of an alien bewilderment:

What if blue just governs the space?
What if my phial becomes a blue canary
or a bush of primroses?

This poem, entitled "The Blue Colour Phial" (1963) can be read as a declaration of an utmost alignment with blue, a colour that is strongly present in Morsi's paintings, a colour that awakens the images of his early youth in Alexandria, a city bordered by the sea.

In 1950 Morsi wrote a poem dedicated to the French poet Paul Valéry, where he painted an image of a woman which would recur fairly consistently in his poetry:

A woman
unlike any other
in a veil that gives away a sunset
Her dark scent unleashes thorns
for a nose without nostrils
Upon the black wall I see her shadow
and it is all red!

In the second half of the 1990s Morsi decided to publish a poetry collection, and that paved the way for more publications. These books reveal a history of exceptional spiritual experiences by the poet who had been living in New York for two decades. At this point in Morsi's career the path of poetry diverges from painting. While New York offered a backdrop to his poems, his paintings remained rooted in the past of an ever blue, and cosmopolitan, Alexandria. Belonging entirely to urban spaces, his poetry, surprisingly, speaks for simplicity and gives voice to the moment of convergence of what is strongly present and yet somehow not fully there.

The Dance. Scratchboard, 24cm x 19cm, 2006.

Keen attentiveness is a crucial aspect of poetry and Morsi takes this element to the extreme. His collection *A Season in Hell: Dress Rehearsal* seems like a scheme for listening, not only to his internal voices but also to objects, places, and manifestations of life. Therefore, sound is a central entry point to Morsi's poetry collection where the reader is shown the way to discovery, not precisely to see what the poet sees, but to pay attention to what the objects say, whether in New York or Alexandria.

Whose voice is this?

Who is howling

at the heart of the latent inferno?

Morsi's inferno is not an extension of Rimbaud's visionary hallucinations. Morsi is least concerned about visions and redemption, his intellectual abyss is rather more subdued so that silence can reign, but also leaves room for cynicism. This silence and subdued expression breaks away with the traditional literary rhetoric of Arabic literature, and in this sense his usage of silence is a rare stylistic feature. Despite Morsi's adherence to traditional prosody his use of language is distinctly free and unconventional. He blends different techniques, including monologue, fable, and storytelling, into a language that is ostensibly simple but it is as enigmatic as silence.

Morsi drew from the pools of figurative art, German expression-ism, and the Italian realism of El Greco. Therefore, it is no surprise that we encounter an evident presence of the figurative in his po-etry, beginning from his poetry collection *Photos from the New York Album*. This tendency continued to feature in his other four poetry collections.

Captivated by urban spaces; alleys, roads, shops, cafés, and city dwellers, Morsi was not interested in constructing his own private space, but rather sought to place the reader at the heart of the urban space / city. This features even in the eulogies he wrote to his friend the Iraqi artist Ardash Kakavian, as well as in his own poem about Edgar Allan Poe's house that was confiscated by New York munici-pality. It is salient to add that Morsi was also keen to stage his scenes in simple language where the elements of the scene are directly named:

What makes you walk alone in Christmas holiday?
Closed is the name of the day
at Soho's cafés, Little Italy's, and even libraries.
What attracts you to shop windows?
Will a poet fall for a manikin?

Morsi writes because he listens attentively:

You were still there
never left the coasts of Purgatory
When a pile of sand fell in the lake of stillness
where birds bathe, all naked
you were naked too in your own silence
When the last ships to exile moved away
in secrecy, from your harbor
boxes are loaded, full of silence!
They will be delivered to islands
sinking in mute labyrinths,
why bother stuffing boxes with silence?

Translated by Najlaa Eltom

AHMED MORSI

Photos from the New York Album

TRANSLATED BY RAPHAEL COHEN

DETAIL FROM A MURAL

For Edwar al-Kharrat

1
Sailors sip bottles of Stella
one after another like mute statues;
the Corniche is thronged with sellers of shellfish from the
    Mediterranean (the White Sea).
Black fish with tired feet
linger in the streets,
exhausted from pounding the asphalt.

Was it evening?
I remember the sky over the Eastern Harbour
was a deaf mirror.
Falling from it are the bodies of the dead.
Were they the bodies of the living?

2
Birds of poetry hover in silence and cunning,
pecking at the café window.

Who bites who?
Did they know
at that very moment you were translating
Laforgue?

                                        20 March 1996

294 E. 48TH ST., NY 10017

1
My advice to those wishing to live in Manhattan
if they fear the pursuit of Death,
crouching in corners, in abandoned apartments,
in the dark labyrinths of washing machines,
in the elevator:
Don't look for a house built before the war.

2
Death lives there among the tenants,
moves about under a mask
that looks like the masks of others
waiting at subway stations.

3
One of the neighbours said,
while I was trying to throw out last week's newspapers
for recycling:
"Would you believe it?
Larry's dead."
It seems my face did not reflect
the expected expressions of grief
and she started talking about Larry
and his wife Linda:
"They were on the West Coast
escaping the perishing cold of New York.
On the way back,
before reaching the gate
he dropped dead on the terminal floor
holding the boarding cards."

4
You usually hear someone – a neighbour – has died
but you never hear a widow weeping
or even know where they've been buried,
if it really mattered to you that is,
and over time I forgot about Larry.

5

I usually get up with the dawn.
After taking a shower, I walk like an automaton
to the locked and bolted door
and fetch the daily newspapers.
Every day I saw him waiting for the elevator
to go for his regular daily jog
before the streets of Manhattan woke up.

6

Larry drank, every evening,
a bottle of French wine.
He wasn't a drunkard
but he loved life.
He frequented the cinema
he frequented restaurants with Linda
like two young lovers, despite the bent back,
the hoarse and cracked voice,
the blonde hair dye.
Did it disguise Linda's real age?

7

The bottles are no longer lined up at midnight
empty as in one of Morandi's still lifes.
No longer does that good man, our neighbour, rise
in the half-light of dawn
to run alone in a city that never sleeps —
a pregnant woman screaming orgasmically
during contractions, morning and night.

8

His wife returned in mourning, without makeup,
though she kept
the dyed-blonde colour of her hair,
determined to defy
the snares of Death
who did not know her address in New York.

Summer by seaside. Acrylic on canvas, 175cm x 155cm, New York City 1985-88

9

The days of mourning did not last long.
It seems Larry had bequeathed his wife Death.
Six months later
she died on another airport floor.

...

My advice to those wishing to live in Manhattan,
if they fear the pursuit of Death,
crouching in corners,
in abandoned apartments,
in the dark labyrinths of washing machines,
in the elevator:
Don't look for a house built before the war.

New York, 1996

THE LADY IN APARTMENT 12E

1

The elevator was crowded one evening
with elderly women,
all dressed up to the nines
their fur coats moth-eaten from poor storage
and the passing of years.
The stooped bodies were slender
but wrinkles on hands and faces
under powder and makeup
sagged under the weight of the years
sagged under the burden of loneliness
and the crushing fear of the unknown.

2

One in a black cloak said:
"Tonight's performance was wonderful.
But Pavarotti, isn't he nearing sixty?"

"He's more than that.
The opera critics who adored his voice
crucified him as soon as he turned sixty."
"Do any of you remember
something she lost once she turned sixty?
Didn't he have a velvety voice
just a few days ago?
Really the *New York Times* critics are so unfair."

3

That rough gravelly voice
is familiar.
Whose is it?
That short, stooped frame
and love of opera?
I recall the nasal twang
I recall the intense gaze of the eyes.

Now, though, in the flurry of personal criticism
which laments for the self as much as for others,
I realised
the one in the black cloak
was my mysterious, timid neighbour.

4

Rachel lived on her own
in a studio apartment next to ours.
She was scared to speak to
or even greet those she chanced upon
in the hallway or by the elevator.
Even Victoria
her cheerful neighbour next door
did not chat with her.
Yet she must have heard
Il Trovatore or Rigoletto
through the wall
or perhaps listened
to the same PBS programs
"Brought to you by Texaco"

many times a year.
Now I wonder in amazement
if that was why
she did not stint in saying hello.

5
One morning
the house shook momentarily
and I heard packing cases.
The question came to mind:
Has someone died?
It was the din of new tenants.

I opened the door abruptly
and worked it out.
Apartment 12E was empty,
no more would the arias of Madame Butterfly
and Nights from the Metropolitan
"Brought to you by Texaco"
be played.
Over time I got used to seeing my young neighbour saying hello
but I was curious to know
where the old woman Rachel
had disappeared to and how she had silently gone?

18 May 1997

THE ROAD TO MANHATTAN

1
From the car that morning Manhattan
loomed in the distance
like tall Giacometti figurines
plucking the fins of fish
submerged in the clouds.
A crazy idea possessed me:
the image had fallen
from my mind onto the ice.

Manhattan was shackled in ice.

2
The picture wasn't bright in any case.
The highway from Queens
crossed neighbourhoods besieged by cities of the dead
strip joints
and brothels advertising Paradise in neon,
admission not by good deeds
but by dollar bills.

Here and there a crumbling church
bears a sign: For sale or to rent.

3
Manhattan slithers forward
stretching dragon hands, smashing drawers
out of which the secrets of poets fall,
like eyeballs in urns of sand and water
and on the threshold of the horizon, skyscrapers
procreate in boredom,
brazenly.
Manhattan approaches naked,
without dyes or masks
to hide her sallow face
in the middle of the day.

4
Long Island City was a shock,
a poke in the eye to a new immigrant.

It was not the gateway to Manhattan,
the Lady of the Atlantic Ocean
the repository of twentieth-century art
exile for Guernica
exile for Les Demoiselles d'Avignon and Max Beckmann
where Marcel Duchamp adopted
a urinal that entered history.

I witnessed for the first time
how neighbourhoods die
and years later
how they come back to life.
The streets, the housing projects,
and hospitals
are the signs of a city of ghosts
abandoned by its inhabitants.
The car slowed down near Queens Bridge.
"Isn't it Sunday?" I wondered.

The bridge was jammed
with cars, and with cyclists
even though they had their own little lane,
but the heralds of Fall
and the brightness of September turned
the rumble of engines
into a choir of singers —
as if all the people
were marching on Manhattan
each in search of something lost.

Was I too
searching for something lost?

5 April 1997

ADVENTURES IN SEARCH OF AL-NIFFARI

1
I combed the streets of Soho, and its bars,
under the polluted streaks of July rain
late, well after midnight,
after the wretched of Bowery Street
had disappeared into the cracks.

I am seeking a lover
one thousand years old.

Waiting for Godot
Acrylic on canvas
152cm x 112cm
New York City 2012

2

It seemed to me while searching
on West Broadway
that I stumbled over a body
but I avoided checking the truth,
averted my face
and continued walking aimlessly,
in my ears a question ringing,
echoing deeply:

Did I stumble over my body
or did I stumble over yours?

12 July 1997

PREPARING TO INTERVIEW AL-NIFFARI

I was struck by the desire to meet you
one day in the Alexandria of Cavafy
but it disappeared, vanished
into the dust of history
the moment my feet touched
the threshold of the ship, and even before it set sail
that desire disappeared into the distance.

Forty years of exile
have passed in lands of deceit
that have taken me far from my city
whenever it seems I'm only
a stone's throw from her shores.

How about meeting
at a mosque in Basra or in New York?
I'd prefer to meet in Manhattan
so you're not shocked at the sight of Basra
naked, stripped of its palm trees.

2

The sad news must have reached you,
that your birthplace Niffar
was stamped out by the feet of time,
and if not for your name
the name would have been written
out of history like so many others.

Permit me, Mawlana,
how long have you lived?
And how will you come?
As an old man or young?
A body or a soul?
By plane or by ship?

Might I suggest to Mawlana,
if you come as a body,
don't wear tenth-century dress
or even twentieth-century.
It's enough to wrap yourself
whether you come evening or morning
in your Mawaqif,* that revelation of mysteries.

18 May 1997

* The Mawaqif of Al-Niffari, who was a 10th-century Sufi mystic, consists of 77
individual 'stations', each in the form of a brief divine revelation addressed to the seeker
whom God has held in that station.

CAFÉ REGGIO

To the poet Joseph Brodsky

I do not remember whether it was morning
or evening
but I recall you were sketching
or writing poetry

or penning a letter to family in Moscow.

You were sitting next to the window, smoking voraciously.
(Only the tobacco companies
knew you were unintentionally
making your shroud.)
The café was empty
apart from a gay couple
in a world of their own
and me, alone, exiled
in the colony of cursed poets,
trying to kill the birds of poetry.

29 November 1997

11 DECEMBER 2004

Today is Saturday,
I think I'll go for a walk down 5th Avenue
which is heaving with life and people
these days.

I was keen to take a camera with me
in case my image slipped away
and disappeared without excuse
in the throng.

I resisted the seduction
of my eyes running away with themselves
behind the women going to and fro
and my gaze being trapped
by electronic snares.
I resisted the longing of the child within me
for our holidays
even though I no longer remember
anything I want to get back,
apart from my mother and father
and all those I've lost for ever.

Suddenly I found myself
on a bench in the middle of Washington Square Park
in my hand a notebook open
to a poem
  in which I saw
      my image.

                              11 December 2004
                              Washington Square Park

MY ALEXANDRIA

1
My first city
I lost
like I lost
my true image
in a secret suitcase
that I forgot to take
with me into exile,
should I say,
or did I bury it deliberately
underground
to draw a new image
without features
to live with in exile
like a false prophet
or a secret fugitive
from a life sentence
in the prison of nothingness
in limbo between silence and wordlessness?

2
My other city
New York
where I've spent a third of a century

with a changeable mask
without features
without identity
has not made me forget my first city,
the one I lost.

3
Alexandria of revelation
and concealment
Alexandria of fragments
in the blood.
My Alexandria,
I rebuilt inside me
all that vanished –
its lighthouse, its treasures –
so it could all vanish
with me for ever.

26 November 2007

Selected and translated
from the collection
Photos from the New York Album,
published in Ahmed Morsi's
Al-'Amal al-Shi'riyya al-Kamila
(Collected Poetic Works),
by the Supreme Council of
Culture, Cairo, 2012.
ISBN 978-9774799520.
www.scc.gov.eg

The 100 best Arabic novels

As a literary magazine dedicated to Arabic literature and its translation, one of our first responsibilities is to follow the literary scene throughout the Arab world and its diaspora. We have noticed in recent years a great rise in the writing of novels, which has been accompanied by the establishment of many awards celebrating Arab literature – the novel in particular.

At the beginning of this year I proposed a special feature of a new list of the best 100 Arabic novels. This proposal was accepted and I was asked to prepare it. After two months working on the project I told the publisher I could not do it. WHY? Because, I found my initial list was full of titles of novels I loved, and therefore it would be Samuel's list, not the sort of list we wanted for the magazine. After much discussion we decided to start with a blank sheet and request nominations for the list from 100 authors, critics, academics, intellectuals and translators. Their nominations would result in Banipal magazine's new list of **The 100 best Arabic novels**. I asked everyone the same question: "In your opinion, which novels do you think deserve to be, or should be, on this new list of the 100 best Arabic novels?" I stressed that the list was for novels, not authors, so there was no restriction on the number of novels that could be nominated for a particular author.

After several months I have gathered together all the responses, and I am delighted to announce here the results. Below are the first five novels, with the full list on the following pages, each has a brief synopsis, and there are short biographies of the authors. If the novel has an English translation, the English title is placed first, followed by transliteration of the Arabic title.

1 *Season of Migration to the North* (*Mawsim al-Hijra ila al-Shamal*) by Tayeb Salih
2 *Cairo Trilogy* (*al-Thulathiyya*) by Naguib Mahfouz
3 *For Bread Alone* (*Al-Khubz al-Hafi*) by Mohamed Choukri
4 *The Secret Life of Saeed The Pessoptimist* (*Al-Waqa'i al-gharibah fi ikhtifa Sa'id Abi al-Nahs al-Mutasha'il*) by Emile Habiby
5 *Children of the Alley* (*Awlad Haretna*) by Naguib Mahfouz

And how is *Season of Migration to the North* the first, you may ask, and not the *Cairo Trilogy*? The nominations have been ranked according to the number received for each title. *Season of Migration to the North* received 61 nominations. Tayeb Salih's other works were: *The Wedding of Zein* and *Daw al-Bayt* (*Bandarshah I*) 3 and *Doumat wad Hamid* 2.

Naguib Mafouz's *Cairo Trilogy* received 41 nominations with eleven other novels also nominated. *Children of the Alley* received 34 (ranked 5); *The Harafish* received 20 (ranked 16); *The Thief and the Dogs* received 15 (ranked 34); *Midaq Alley* 12 (ranked 49); *Miramar* 10 (ranked 70); *Adrift on the Nile* 9 (ranked 80); and six other novels each nominated two or three times. Overall, looking at these two authors, not their works, Naguib Mahfouz received 106 nominations and Tayeb Salih 69. Let me follow through the nominations of a few other titles. Number 3 is *For Bread Alone,* the only novel of Mohamed Choukri, which received 37 nominations, while number 4, *The Secret Life of Saeed The Pessoptimist* by Emile Habiby, received 36 nominations and another novel of Habiby, *Ikhtiya*, received just 1.

Number 6 is *Zayni Barakat* by Gamal al-Ghitani with 34 nominations, while two other works of al-Ghitani, *The Zafarani Files* and *Kitab Al Tagaliyat,* received 4 each.

Cities of Salt by Abdelrahman Munif is number 7, with 33 nominations. Eight other novels by him were nominated: *Sharq al-Mutawassit* (East of the Mediterranean) received 20 and is ranked 17; *Al-Ashjar wa-Ightiyal Marzouq* (The Trees and the Assassination of Marzouq) received 9 and is ranked 77; and the other six received 1 or 2 nominations each.

The Arab Writers' Union published a list of 100 (actually 105) best Arabic novels in 2001. *Banipal*'s new list shares 44 titles, but includes another 35 novels that did not make the AWU list, and 21 titles published after 2001, representing the new generation of novelists. These latter include *Frankenstein in Baghdad* by Ahmed Saadawi, ranked 15; *Papa Sartre* by Ali Bader, ranked 22; *In Praise of Hatred* by Khaled Khalifa, ranked 44 and *The Bamboo Stalk*, ranked 47.

In looking at the results, a question immediately leaps out: why are well-known novelists such as Wacini Laradj, Ibrahim Nasrallah, Amir Tag Elsir and Lutfiya al-Dulaimi, missing from the list? In fact, ten novels of Wacini Laredj are nominated, but each one only 2 or 3 times. None achieved the minimum number of 9 nominations. Similarly with novels by Ibrahim Nasrallah: five of his novels are nominated but each less than 9 times – *Time of White Horses* received 4; *Dog War II*, which won the 2018 IPAF, received 3; and the other three novels received 1 and 2 nominations each. What conclusion can we draw from this? The results appear to show that if an author has a single masterpiece, then that has been nominated. If not, then nominations are scattered among the author's many titles.

Let us look at the nominated titles of other well-known authors. Ibrahim Abdel Meguid, for example, had 6 novels nominated: *No One Sleeps in Alexandria* received 23 nominations (and is ranked 14), whereas *The Other Place* received 4, *Birds of Amber* 3, and three novels, *The House of Jasmine*, *Atabat al-Bahja* and *Adagio*, each received 1 nomination. Another example is Ghada Samman, who has 5 novels nominated: *Beirut Nightmares* has 10 nominations (ranked 71), and there are four outside the 100 – *The Night of the First Billion* with 2 nominations, and three with 1 nomination each: *La Bahr Fi Bayrut* (No Sea in Beirut), *Al Ruayah Al Mustahilah: Fasifasa' Dimashqiya* (The Impossible Novel: Damascene Mosaic), and *Al-Jasad Haqibat Safer* (The body suitcase).

Hoda Barakat received a total of 27 nominations for 6 novels: *The Stone of Laughter* received 11, *Disciples of Passion* 9, *Tiller of Waters* 4, and three other novels 1 each – *Sayyidi wa Habibi* (My Master and My Love), *Bareed al-Layl* (Night Post) and *Malakout hathihi al-Ard* (Kingdom of this land). Four novels of Hanan al-Shakyh were nominated: The *Story of Zahra* received 15 nominations (ranked 27), *The Locust and the Bird* 5, *Misk al-Ghazaal* (Scent of a Ghazelle) 4 and *Beirut Blues* 2.

I leave you now to read through the titles and authors at your leisure, and explore other facts and figures about the list.

Samuel Shimon

1 Season of Migration to the North (Mawsim al-Hijra ila al-Shamal) by Tayeb Salih (1966)

Described as the most important Arab novel of the twentieth century, *Season of Migration to the North* depicts the lasting effects of colonialism on contemporary Sudanese society. Set in 1960s Sudan, events are narrated by an unnamed man who, after studying for some time in England, returns to his native village in rural Sudan with hopes of using his Western education to some benefit. However, the narrator is intrigued by an enigmatic new face in the village, Mustafa Sa'eed, becoming aware, as the latter's alarming past unfolds, that their experiences are more connected than he could have imagined . . .

Tayeb Salih (1929–2009) was born in Karmakol in the Northern Province of Sudan and educated at the University of Khartoum. He moved to London to study and worked abroad for many years, including with the Ministry of Information in Qatar and UNESCO in Paris. *Season of Migration to the North* was published in 1966 and won international acclaim. It is one of the most influential Arabic novels of the 20th century.

2 Cairo Trilogy (al-Thulathiyya) by Naguib Mahfouz (1956-57)

One of the most celebrated works of Mahfouz's career, this trilogy comprises Palace Walk (1956), Palace of Desire (1957) and Sugar Street (1957), all of which are real street names in Cairo – the setting for the three novels. Through the lens of one family, that of Al-Sayyid Ahmad 'Abd al-Jawad, a well-off Cairene merchant, the trilogy traces the turbulent period in Egypt's history spanning from 1919 – the year of the revolution against the British colonial powers in Egypt – to 1944 and the close of the Second World War.

Naguib Mahfouz (1911–2006) was born in the Gamaliya district of Cairo and began writing when he was seventeen. He began his literary career with short stories and historical novels, and his contribution to the Arabic novel earned him global renown, seeing him win the Nobel Prize for Literature in 1988. His long and prolific literary career produced 34 novels, countless short stories, mostly set in Cairo, and many film scripts. He is celebrated today as one of the pioneers of modern Arabic literature.

3 For Bread Alone (Al-Khubz al-Hafi) by Mohamed Choukri (1982)

Mohamed Choukri's famed work is an astonishing and candid account of his early life in Morocco. Beginning from the famine which drove his family from their home in the Rif to Tangier, Choukri describes the struggle to survive amidst a society rife with danger and poverty, not to mention the violent rages of his vicious father. Unable to find steady work, he plunges into the simultaneously thrilling and horrifying depths of a world of sex, crime and drugs, until a chance encounter in prison changes the course of his life forever . . .

Mohamed Choukri (1935-2003) is one of North Africa's most renowned authors. Born in Beni Chiker village in the Rif Mountains during a devastating famine, Choukri recounts his turbulent childhood in his celebrated and sometime controversial autobiography, *For Bread Alone* (al-Khubz al-Hafi). At the age of twenty he learned to read and write, publishing his first short story in 1966. He went on to pursue a literary and teaching career, writing three novels and later being awarded the chair of Arabic Literature at Ibn Battuta College, Tangier.

4 The Secret Life of Saeed The Pessoptimist (Al-Waqa'i al-gharibah fi ikhtifa Sa'id Abi al-Nahs al-Mutasha'il) by Emile Habiby (1974)

Through the character of the gullible, even comic Saeed, Habiby powerfully depicts the political reality of the post-1948 Palestinian experience in this modern classic. Saeed is a Palestinian who becomes an Israeli citizen and informer, narrating his experience of the suffering and hardships encountered by Arabs in Israel through a series of letters to an Israeli newspaper. The absurdity of Saeed's revelations (in which he claims to have communicated with aliens) gives this satirical masterpiece all the more sting in its political and historical context.

Emile Habiby (1922–1996), born in Haifa, Palestine, pursued a career in politics before writing his celebrated works of fiction. Soon after the creation of Israel, he founded what later became the Israeli Communist Party, Rakah, serving as a member in the Israeli parliament for twenty years. The profound insight his novels offer into the Arab experience in Israel earned him great acclaim as a writer, and he was awarded the Al-Quds Prize from the PLO in 1990, and the Israeli Prize for Arabic Literature in 1992.

5 Children of the Alley (Awlad Haretna) by Naguib Mahfouz (1959)

Originally published as a newspaper serial, *Children of our Alley* (or, alternatively, *Children of Gebelawi*) is considered one of the most controversial of Mahfouz's works. It weaves together the stories of the inhabitants of an imaginary nineteenth-century alley in Cairo, ruled over by the tyrannical Gebelawi. The reinvention of Abrahamic religious figures in the protagonists of the

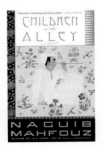

novel, such as Moses and the prophet Mohammad, has earned it both criticism and praise as a striking metaphor for the interlinked histories of Judaism, Christianity and Islam.

6 Zayni Barakat by Gamal al-Ghitani (1974)

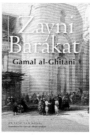

Egypt, 1516: the Mamluk dynasty is on the brink of collapse with the advance of the invading Ottomans. Through multiple sources, ranging from official communiques to personal accounts, the novel traces the rise to power of the enigmatic, controversial and puritanical Zayni Barakat, holder of the prestigious Mamluk office of Muhtasib, Inspectorship of Markets. His control over the corrupt city of Cairo (almost a character itself) is both exerted and thwarted through a complex web of intrigue and espionage, which led to the work being seen as a powerful allegorical critique of authoritarianism.

Gamal al-Ghitani (1945–2015) was one of Egypt's leading novelists of the modern era. Born in the Sohag Governorate of Upper Egypt, he originally trained as a carpet designer. However, in 1969 he began to focus on writing, becoming a journalist for the Egyptian newspaper *Akhbar al-Yawm*. His novel *Zayni Barakat* brought him international acclaim. He was editor-in-chief of the Cairo *Akhbar al-Adab* literary weekly, and a consulting editor of *Banipal* magazine for many years. In 2009 he won the prestigious Sheikh Zayed Book Award.

7 Cities of Salt (Mudun al-Milh) by Abdelrahman Munif (1984)

Cities of Salt marks the first in a five-volume series of novels. Set in an unnamed country in the Arabian Peninsula in the 1930s, the novel explores the far-reaching political and social consequences of the discovery of oil in a poor oasis community.

Told from the perspective of the community's Bedouin inhabitants over the course of many years, *Cities of Salt* attracted both praise and controversy, being an expression of many of the issues experienced by Gulf countries in the twentieth century.

Abdelrahman Munif (1933–2004) was a Jordanian-born Saudi novelist who lived most of his life in exile. He received a PhD in oil economics from the University of Belgrade. Among his novels he is best known for his *Cities of Salt* series, largely influenced by his earlier experience of working in politics and the oil industry. A number of his works were banned in Saudi Arabia due to their strong political criticism, and his Saudi citizenship was eventually revoked.

8 In Search of Walid Masoud (Al-Bahth an Walid Masoud) by Jabra Ibrahim Jabra (1978)

This novel follows the disappearance of Palestinian activist and writer Walid Masoud. After his tape recorder and his car are found, his friends and enemies start reminiscing about Walid as a man and a committed idealist. The result is a complex and symbolic portrayal of an Arab intellectual in the postcolonial era, who took the Palestinian cause to heart and tried to avoid falling into the traps of factionalism. Political commitment and memory are two topics Jabra reiterates in his novels.

Jabra Ibrahim Jabra (1920–1994) was a Palestinian novelist, poet, painter and translator. After his studies at Exeter, Cambridge and Harvard universities, he settled in Iraq in 1948 and never returned to occupied Palestine. He translated works by Shakespeare, William Faulkner, T. S. Eliot and Samuel Beckett into Arabic. He was actively involved in a community of artists who went on to create the Hurufiyya Movement which sought to combine traditional Islamic art and modern art. He published around 70 books: novels, memoirs and translations.

9 Rama and the Dragon (Rama wal-Tinnin) by Edwar al-Kharrat (1980)

Rama and the Dragon represents a ground-breaking contribution to narrative discourse in Arabic fiction, acclaimed as "experimental". Set in Egypt of the 1960s and 1970s, it presents a non-linear series of scenes, memories and dialogues, framed by a love story between the protagonists – Mikhail, a Coptic Christian, and Rama, a Muslim woman. Through these two characters al-Kharrat juxtaposes the worldviews which beset Egypt, weaving allusions to the rich Arabic literary, philosophical and cultural heritage into the text, and simultaneously creating a work which relates to human nature on a universal level.

Edwar al-Kharrat (1926–2015), novelist, critic and translator, was born in Alexandria into a Coptic Christian family. Whilst he published his first collection of short stories, *High Walls*, in 1959, it was not until twenty years later that his highly acclaimed and extraordinary novel *Rama and the Dragon* was published. He received several prestigious literary awards, including the Naguib Mahfouz Medal for Literature, was founder editor of the literary magazine of *Gallery 68*, and is commemorated as one of the leading figures among the renowned Sixties Generation of Egyptian writers.

10 Gate of the Sun (Bab al-Shams) by Elias Khoury (1998)

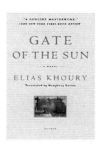

In a compelling rendition of the *Thousand and One Nights* narrative style, this novel recounts the many interwoven stories of Palestinians expelled from Galilee after the 1948 Nakba. The setting is a makeshift hospital in Shatila camp, Beirut, where Khalil sits at the bedside of his comatose patient Yunes, an early freedom fighter, beginning to tell a story in an attempt to save him. Yet as one story branches out into dozens of individual tales, stretching across time and space, social and political context, a vivid and moving history of the Palestinian people emerges.

Elias Khoury is an award-winning novelist, playwright, journalist, academic and literary critic. He was born in Beirut in 1948 and studied there and in Paris, returning to Lebanon during the civil war and serving on the editorial board of several publications. He was editor-in-chief of *Al-Mulhaq*, cultural supplement of *An-Nahar* newspaper, has held academic positions at universities in Lebanon and the US. He is editor of the Arabic edition of the Institute of Palestine Studies journal. He has published eleven novels and his work has been translated into many languages.

11 Men in the Sun (Rijal fi al-Shams) by Ghassan Kanafani (1963)

Kanafani's novella follows three Palestinian refugees, Abu Qais, Asad and Marwan, as they attempt to cross the border from Iraq to Kuwait in order to find employment. As memories and flashbacks reveal the separate pasts of the three men, now united by their struggle to secure the conditions to be smuggled into Kuwait, Kanafani presents the harsh and poignant reality of the  many dimensions of Palestinian exile and suffering post-1948. The novella was adapted by Tewfik Saleh into the film, *The Dupes*, in 1972.

Ghassan Kanafani (1936–1972) was born in Akka, Palestine, his family fleeing to Syria in 1948. He lived in Kuwait for a period before moving to Lebanon in 1960. There Kanafani pursued his career as a writer and political activist, becoming spokesman for the Popular Front for the Liberation of Palestine. He was assassinated in Beirut. His passionate commitment to the Palestinian cause shines through his works and he is considered among the most influential Arab writers of the modern era.

12 Seeds of Corruption (Fasad al-Amkina) by Sabri Moussa (1973)

Seeds of Corruption tells the story of Nicola, a Russian traveller who leaves his wife and daughter behind to work on the first mining site of al-Darhib Mountain in Egypt's eastern desert. Through his friendship with Issa, a Bedouin who works as a guide to the foreign workers, Nicola begins to learn about the culture and rituals of the desert communities – a knowledge which only intensifies the tragic nature of the corruption of their lives and surroundings by the very external forces that he himself represents.

Sabri Moussa (1932–2018) was born in Damietta, Egypt, where he studied painting and worked as a teacher. He began writing in the 1950s, publishing four collections of short stories, three novels, three travel books and scripts for ten major Egyptian films, some of which, such as *Al-Boustagi* (The Postman), are now considered classics. He also helped to found *Sabah el-Kheir* weekly magazine and was awarded several Egyptian state literary prizes, as well as the Pegasus Prize for Literature in 1978.

13 The Heron (Malik al-Hazin) by Ibrahim Aslan (1992)

Set on the eve of the January 1977 bread riots, the popular uprising against IMF austerity programmes and privatization that nearly overthrew President Anwar Sadat, Aslan's celebrated novel revolves around life in the Cairo neighbourhood of Kit Kat. Whilst young

writer Youssef al-Naggar is central to the narrative, the novel intricately delves into the lives of an astounding number of characters from the neighbourhood, all of whom are preoccupied by their own concerns and individual sense of estrangement. It was adapted into the major film Kit Kat by Daoud Abdel Sayed in 1991.

Ibrahim Aslan (1935–2012) was born in Tanta, Egypt. He published his first collection of short stories, *Buhayrat al-Misa'* (The Evening Lake), in 1972, and his first novel, The Heron, in 1983. He was also cultural editor at the Cairo bureau of *Al-Hayat* newspaper. Aslan became one of Egypt's leading novelists and short story writers, and was awarded numerous literary prizes, including the Sawiris Prize in 2006.

14 No One Sleeps in Alexandria (La Ahad Yanam fi al-Iskandariyya) by Ibrahim Abdel Meguid (1996)

The first in his trilogy about Alexandria, this novel explores the interconnected lives of an assortment of the city's inhabitants as they are shaken by the outbreak of the Second World War. The pivot for these many individual stories is the remarkable friendship between Sheikh Magd al-Din, a devout Muslim originally from northern Egypt, and Dimyan, a Coptic Christian from the south: a relationship which not only captures in rich detail daily life in

Alexandria during this period, but also the essence of a city marked

throughout history by its cultural vibrancy and diversity.

Ibrahim Abdel Meguid was born in Alexandria in 1946. He graduated from Alexandria University with a degree in philosophy in 1973, moving to Cairo shortly after to pursue a literary career. He has published many novels and short story collections, some of which have been translated into English and French, and has been awarded a number of prestigious literary prizes, including the Naguib Mahfouz Medal (1996), the Egyptian State Prize (2007), the Sawiris Prize (2011), and the Sheikh Zayed Book Award (2016).

15 Frankenstein in Baghdad (Frankinshtaiyn fi Baghdad) by Ahmed Saadawi (2013)

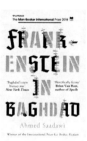

In this vivid and absurdist morality tale, set in 2005 in the rundown Bataween district of Baghdad, protagonist Hadi al-Attag collects the body parts he finds in the street and puts them together to create a "new man", the Whatsitsname. Once it is complete, the creature sets out to avenge all those whose body parts he is made out of. The search to track down the unearthly monster (or saviour, as some view him) behind the murders ensues as the Whatsitsname struggles to keep his made-up body intact after each killing, noting that his body is the mix of the diverse backgrounds that the Iraqi state itself has never achieved.

Ahmed Saadawi, born in Baghdad in 1973, is a novelist, poet, journalist, screenwriter and documentary filmmaker for TV. In addition to one collection of poetry and one of short stories, he has three novels, *The Beautiful Country* (2004), *Indeed he Dreams of Plays or Dies* (2008) and *Frankenstein in Baghdad* (2013), which won the 2014 International Prize for Arabic Fiction (IPAF) and was shortlisted for the 2018 Man Booker International Prize. In 2010 he was selected for the Beirut39 project, as one of the best Arab authors below the age of forty.

16 The Harafish (Malhamat al-Harafish) by Naguib Mahfouz (1977)

A thrilling epic on the weaknesses of human nature, *The Harafish* documents episodes in the dramatic rise and fall of a prominent family in a timeless urban Egyptian society. Beginning with the exemplary clan leader Ashur al-Nagi, the novel witnesses over many generations the deviance of the al-Nagi family from their predecessor's legendary reputation, and the tales of love, death, intrigue and passion which mark these vibrant characters' bids to reclaim the honour of the al-Nagi name.

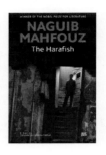

17 Sharq al-Mutawassit (East of the Mediterranean) by Abdelrahman Munif (1975)

Set in an unnamed country in the Middle East where the regime is quashing basic human rights, a brother and a sister, Rajab and Aneesa, are each imprisoned in their own way. He is locked in a cell where he is physically and psychologically tortured. She is captive to her own home, oppressed and angry. Through a series of flashbacks and internal monologue, the siblings discuss their past and the choices they made, offering a male and a female perspective to a crisis.

18 The Long Way Back (al-Raj' al-Ba'id) by Fuad al-Takarli (1980)

A bold and remarkable reflection on modern Iraqi political history, *The Long Way Back* is set in the days and weeks preceding the overthrow of prime minister Abd al-Karim Qasim in 1963. The reader is drawn into the world of the Ismaili family: four generations living under one roof, in an old house in the Bab al-Shaykh neighbourhood of Baghdad. Through the intertwined stories of the family members, we observe how their private disputes and passions come to collide dramatically with the wider political turmoil around them.

Fuad al-Takarli (1927–2008) was one of Iraq's pioneering fiction writers of the 20th century. Born in Baghdad, he studied Law at Baghdad University and went on to work in the Justice Ministry, becoming a judge in 1956. Although he began writing it in 1966, his masterpiece novel *The Long Way Back* was not published until 1980 in Beirut. He retired from the law in 1983 to focus on his writing, winning the prestigious Al Owais award for the Arabic novel in 2000.

19 Walimah li-A'shaab al-Bahr (A Banquet for Seaweed) by Haidar Haidar (1983)

The most renowned and controversial of Haidar's works, *A Banquet for Seaweed* moves between Iraq and Algeria as both countries witness the drastic political upheaval which follows the end of colonial rule. Mahdi Jawad is a disillusioned member of the Iraqi Communist Party who flees the Baathist regime in the 1970s to the Algerian town of Buna, only to be confronted with the harsh reality of the Boumédiène military dictatorship. This novel powerfully recreates the widespread suffering and desperation which characterizes this critical moment in the history of both countries.

Haidar Haidar was born in 1936 in the village of Husain al-Bahr in Syria. He first began writing fiction in the 1960s, publishing short stories in literary journals. In the 1970s he worked as a teacher in Algeria, before moving to Lebanon to work as a journalist and editor. His novels and short stories are marked by their daring exploration of taboo themes in the Arab world. He currently lives in Syria.

20 Zaat by Sonallah Ibrahim (1992)

Zaat is a girl from lower-middle class Cairo whose life revolves

around her marriage, her neighbours, and gossip. Ibrahim describes her life in tragicomic tones, while also pouring scorn on a society preoccupied with Western consumerism – exemplified by Zaat herself, who passionately desires a deep-freeze and European furniture. Zaat's story is told against the background of the history of Egypt under Nasser, Sadat and Mubarak, and the novel incorporates news reports of, among other things, military losses on the Sinai peninsula, contaminated food imported from Chernobyl, the rise in prices of basic commodities, and company bankruptcies – all pointing to a country on the verge of collapse.

Sonallah Ibrahim (b.1937) is an Egyptian novelist and short-story writer associated with other authors of the 'Sixties Generation'. Many of his works focus on aspects of Egyptian society and on foreign interference in the region – about which he is highly critical – though he has also demonstrated wider interests: *Beirut, Beirut* deals with the civil war in Lebanon, and *Warda* with the Dhofar Rebellion, for example. Ibrahim's works have often been censored, and in 1959 he was imprisoned for his left-wing political views. Ibrahim was awarded the Ibn Rushd Prize for Freedom of Thought in 2004, in Berlin.

21 Al-Nakhla wal-Jiran (The Palm Tree and the Neighbours) by Ghaib Tu'ma Farman (1965)

This novel provides a rare and moving insight into the effects of the Second World War on the Iraqi people. Centred in the lower and middle-class quarter of al-Murabba'a in Baghdad, it follows the everyday lives of its inhabitants as they try to persevere amidst desperate poverty and a prevailing atmosphere of disillusionment and despair, poignantly symbolized in the withering of the quarter's only palm tree. Farman's vivid and realistic depictions of

neighbourhood personalities, their lives and their language, open a forgotten moment in the history of the Iraqi people. It was a roaring success after being adapted and performed as a play.

Ghaib Tu'ma Farman (1927–1990), born in Baghdad, was one of Iraq's best-known novelists. Sometimes called the author of the first Iraqi modern novel, he made a decisive contribution to the Iraqi novel's development. He received his BA from Baghdad University in 1955. His short stories and numerous novels, characterized by their focus on social issues affecting Iraq between the 1940s and 1970s, were all published after his emigration to Moscow in 1960, where he spent the rest of his life. He was an acclaimed journalist and translator of Russian literature into Arabic. His work remains untranslated into English.

22 Papa Sartre (Baba Sartre) by Ali Bader (2001)

A penniless academic is commissioned by two questionable individuals to write a biography of the Iraqi existentialist philosopher Abd al-Rahman, the celebrated "Sartre of Baghdad". Yet as the biographer starts to piece together fragments of Abd al-Rahman's life, he soon finds himself uncovering the disturbing truth of this famed figure's intellectual pretentions and hedonistic lifestyle. A fascinating and frequently critical glance at the vibrant intellectual scene of 1960s Baghdad.

Ali Bader is an Iraqi novelist, journalist and poet. Born in 1964 in Baghdad, he studied western philosophy and French literature at university. He has published over 20 works of fiction, poetry and criticism, and has received a number of awards for his novels, such as the State Prize for Literature in Baghdad (2002), as well as being longlisted twice for the International Prize for Arabic Fiction. He currently lives in Belgium.

23 The Granada Trilogy (Thulathiyat Gharnata) by Radwa Ashour (1994–95)

Spanning from the fall of the last Islamic kingdom of Granada in 1491 to the expulsion of the Arabs of Al-Andalus in 1609, Radwa Ashour's master-piece chronicles the lives of three generations of a Spanish Arab family. Witnessing a time of intense persecution of their religion and culture, the novel presents a colourful and touching image of the everyday lives of bookbinder Abu Jafaar and his offspring, who continue to find pockets of joy amidst the turmoil which surrounds them . . .

Radwa Ashour (1946–2014) was an Egyptian novelist, critic and professor of English literature. Born in Cairo to a family with strong literary ties, she graduated in 1967 from university there with a BA in comparative literature and later received a PhD from the University of Massachusetts. In her exceptional literary career, she published eight novels, two collections of short stories, five works of criticism and an autobiography, as well as lecturing at Ain Shams University, Cairo. Awards she received for her literary works include the 2007 Constantine Cavafy Prize for Literature.

24 Al-Yater (The Anchor) by Hanna Mina (1975)

This novel recounts the story of a 19th century sailor, Zakaria Mersenelli, who has committed a murder and becomes a fugitive, hiding in a forest in desolate isolation. With a growing awareness of conscience, the isolation allows him the chance for introspection in nature, for understanding what it is to be a man, and for the discovery of love. The woman he meets helps to transform him, and rid him of his animality through repentance.

Hanna Mina (1924–2018) was a pioneer of social realism in Arabic fiction and a writer with a passionate concern for changing the existing order of Arab society. He was self-taught and worked at a great variety of jobs: porter, stevedore, sailor, barber, and journalist, as well as living on the streets. After a period in Beirut, he moved to Damascus. In 1951 he co-founded the Syrian Writers Federation and began his literary career with his first novel, *Blue Lamps*, out in 1954. He wrote about 40 novels and several short story collections. In 2005 he was awarded the Arab Writers' Prize and in 2010 the Mohamed Zafzaf Prize for Arabic Literature. Only two of his novels are translated into English.

25 The Lamp of Umm Hashim (Qandil Umm Hashim) by Yahya Hakki (1943)

Having been sent to England to complete his studies in medicine, Ismail returns to his native Egypt. However, when he tries to establish himself as a physician in the intensely religious and conservative Cairo neighbourhood of Umm Hashim where he grew up, he finds himself unable to relate to anything. Often compared with Tayeb Salih's *Season of Migration to the North*, this is the story of a young man who struggles to reconcile his new belief system with the traditional values of his own culture, and the decisions he ultimately has to make in order to overcome this internal conflict.

Yahya Hakki (1905–1992) was born in Cairo to a family of Turkish ancestry. He originally trained as a lawyer, joining the diplomatic service in 1928 and being posted to countries such as Turkey, France and Italy. Publishing his first short story at the age of 20, he is considered a pioneer of the Arabic short story. He published four collections of stories, one novel, and many articles, as well as translating literary works into Arabic and becoming editor of *Al-Majalla* magazine 1961–71.

26 Love in Exile (Al-Hub fi al-Manfa) by Bahaa Taher (1995)

An Egyptian journalist ends up in a self-imposed exile in a European city after refusing to renounce his Nasserist beliefs and divorcing his wife. Yet his fresh start overseas is quickly shaken, both by the horrific news of the massacre of Palestinians in Lebanon in 1982 and by his unlikely love affair with Brigette, an Austrian woman much younger than himself. Taher intricately explores the many dimensions of exile and its impact on the human mind in this engrossing and memorable novel.

Bahaa Taher, the celebrated Egyptian author, was born in Cairo in 1935. After graduating in literature from the University of Cairo, he began a career in radio broadcasting with Egypt's Radio 2. In 1964 he published his first short story and became involved in the Gallery 68 movement, and has published novels, short story collections and non-fiction works. Political repression in the 1970s under the Sadat administration led him to relocate to Switzerland as a UN translator. He subsequently returned to Egypt, where he received the State's Award of Merit in Literature in 1998 and the International Prize for Arabic Fiction Award in 2008.

27 The Story of Zahra (Hikayat Zahra) by Hanan al-Shakyh (1980)

This tells the stunning and provocative journey of Zahra, a young Lebanese woman whose search for her identity is riddled with the complexities of patriarchal traditions in society. When a series of tragic events drive Zahra to flee to her uncle in West Africa, she finds herself similarly compromised by her vulnerability, and returns some time later to a war-torn Beirut. However, the form of love which she encounters here will eventually force Zahra to pay the price . . .

Hanan al-Shaykh is an award-winning novelist, journalist and playwright. She was born and grew up in Lebanon, moving to Cairo when she was a teenager and writing her first novel there. She returned to Beirut to work for *An-Nahar* newspaper until 1975, moving to Saudi Arabia before settling in London, where she still lives.

28 Fuqaha' al-Dhalam (The Sages of Darkness) by Salim Barakat (1985)

In a Kurdish village in Northern Syria, a son named Bekas is born to Mullah Binaff. Bekas's instant ability to speak is considered a miracle, however this supernatural power to defy the boundaries of time soon takes on an alarming form, as Bekas starts to age throughout the course of the day, ending up an old man by sunset. This tale, a testament to Barakat's innovative style, explores the plight of the Kurdish people through the dimension of mysticism and folklore.

Salim Barakat is a Kurdish-Syrian novelist and poet, born in 1951 in Qamishli, Syria. In 1970 he went to Damascus to study Arabic literature but moved to Beirut shortly after, where he published various works of poetry, two novels, a diary and two autobiographical volumes. He then moved to Cyprus, working as associate editor of the prestigious Palestinian magazine *Al-Karmel* and publishing more volumes of poetry and novels In 1999 he settled in Sweden, where he still lives, writing and publishing his works. Barakat's literary style is especially noted for its complex and innovative features.

29 Druz Bilghrad: Hikayat Hanna Yaqub (The Druze of Belgrade) by Rabee Jaber (2010)

Set in the aftermath of the bloody civil war of Mount Lebanon in 1860, the novel follows a group of Lebanese Druze fighters who are exiled to Belgrade as punishment for their involvement. Among them is also the Christian Hana Yacoub, an unfortunate egg-seller who ends up being the victim of a prisoner exchange with one of their fellow Druze fighters. Spanning across many years, *The Druze of Belgrade* narrates the trials and misadventures of these men as they traverse the Balkan lands in their struggle to survive.

Rabee Jaber is a Lebanese novelist and journalist. Born in 1972, he studied Physics at the American University of Beirut. He published his first novel, *Sayed al-Atma* (Master of Darkness), at the age of twenty. Since then he has published numerous works of fiction, including *The Druze of Belgrade*, for which he was awarded the 2012 International Prize for Arabic Fiction. He was editor of *Afaaq* (Horizons), the weekly cultural supplement of *Al-Hayat* newspaper.

30 Return of the Spirit ('Awdat al-Ruh) by Tawfiq al-Hakim (1933)

Return of the Spirit chronicles the life of a young middle-class Egyptian and his extended family, and how this is affected by the outbreak of the 1919 Revolution. Through the intricacies of daily life, ranging from humorous social situations to the sting of failed romantic endeavours, al-Hakim paints a vibrant image of Egyptian culture and society which is echoed in the political backdrop of events: Egypt's monumental revival of its national conscience.

Tawfiq al-Hakim (1898–1987) was born in Alexandria, Egypt. He studied law in Cairo, moving to Paris to continue his studies but returning to Egypt much earlier than anticipated in 1928. He began working for the Ministry of Justice in Alexandria and other cities, however in 1936 he abandoned his legal career to devote himself to writing. Though his oeuvre includes novels, poems and essays, he is best remembered for his numerous plays, and is considered a pioneer of modern Arabic drama.

31 Al-Shira' wal-Asifa (The Sail and the Storm) by Hanna Mina (1966)

Based on the author's personal experiences at sea, *The Sail and the Storm* is set in a small coastal town in Syria during the Second World War. At the heart of the story is al-Tarawsi, a spirited man who, despite his humble means, manages to fulfil his dream of going to sea. Yet the merciless sea sends all kinds of waves crashing into al-Tarawsi's life. This novel strikingly captures the adventure, perils and determination which characterise the life of a sailor, ultimately evoking man's constant struggle to overcome nature.

32 The Yacoubian Building (Imarat Yaqoubyan) by Alaa Al Aswany (2002)

Once an architectural jewel of downtown Cairo, the Yacoubian Building has become a crumbling relic. Inside the derelict building, a new breed of occupants has also been witnessed: Cairo's social elite has been replaced with a hotchpotch of characters, their backgrounds as diverse as their flaws. This novel peers into the lives of the Yacoubian Building residents, threading their separate tales of love, power, sex, corruption and despair into one dramatic finale. Adapted as a film by Marwan Hamed in 2006, this bestselling novel is a revealing insight into contemporary Egyptian society.

Alaa Al Aswany is a bestselling Egyptian writer. Born in Cairo in 1957, he attended the French Lycée and went on to study dentistry at Cairo University and the University of Illinois. He has published short stories, novels, plays and articles on politics and literature. He has received many awards for his literary works.

33 Azazeel by Youssef Ziedan (2008)

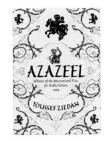

Set in the fifth century, *Azazeel* traces the journey of doctor-monk Hypa across Egypt and Syria, searching for spiritual enlightenment amidst the violent upheaval of the early Eastern Church. Tormented as much by his own desires as he is by the brutal scenes he witnesses on his travels, Hypa is beset by an inner struggle against his devil Azazeel, the inescapable barrier to his religious aspirations. The English translation was joint winner of the 2013 Saif Ghobash Banipal Translation Prize.

Youssef Ziedan is a renowned Egyptian scholar and writer. Born in 1958 in Sohag Governorate, he moved to Alexandria at a young age and graduated from the philosophy department at the University of Alexandria. He held the post of professor of Islamic Philosophy and was Director of the Manuscript Centre and Museum at the Library of Alexandria. *Azazeel* won the 2009 IPAF Prize. In addition to his novels, he has published numerous academic volumes relating to Islamic philosophy, Sufism and medicine, and catalogued eleven Egyptian manuscript libraries.

34 The Thief and the Dogs (Al-Liss wal-Kilab) by Naguib Mahfouz (1980)

Mahfouz's acclaimed novella is a vivid insight into the psychological state of a man driven by his bitterness and desire for vengeance. Recently released from prison after a four-year sentence, young thief

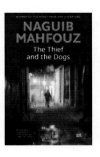

Said Mahran is confronted with disturbing changes at both a personal level (his wife's betrayal with a close friend) and in society at large, adapting to a new, post-revolutionary Egypt. Consumed by disillusionment and despair, Said's initial need to settle his personal grievances develops into a full-blown war against society, with little to protect him from the consequences of his crazed determination to exact justice.

35 Al-Hayy al-Latini (The Latin Quarter) by Suhail Idriss (1989)

Suhail Idriss's renowned novel documents the experience of a young Lebanese student who journeys to Paris during the 1950s to complete a doctorate in literature. As he and his friends of the Latin Quarter readily immerse themselves in the profoundly different world they encounter there, he finds himself tormented by his inability to reconcile this with his previous life in Beirut.

Suhail Idriss (1925–2008) was a Lebanese novelist, translator, lexicographer and publisher. After being educated in Beirut, he went on to study in France, gaining a PhD in literature from the Sorbonne in 1952. He published three novels, six short story collections and translated numerous works, he is the founder of the major literary periodical *Al-Adab* in 1953, and later the publishing house Dar al-Adab, both based in Beirut.

36 Gold Dust (Al-Tibr) by Ibrahim al-Koni (1990)

The relationship of a Bedouin chieftain's son Ukhayyad with his thoroughbred camel is at the core of this novel. Growing up together, in a life harsh and precarious they develop a physical interdependency and communion. This almost spiritual bond between Ukhayyad and his camel creates a confrontation with social customs. When he is asked to choose between his camel and family, Ukhayyad abandons his tribe, where the lust for gold seems to have taken over traditional values.

Ibrahim al-Koni (b. 1948) grew up in the desert of the Tuareg, Libya, and only started to read and write at the age of twelve. He studied comparative literature in Moscow and worked as a journalist in Moscow and Warsaw. In 1993 he settled in Switzerland. A prolific author of over 80 works, including short stories, poems and over 60 novels, with translations into 35 languages, his writings mainly turn on Tuareg life, culture, legends and myths.

37 The Open Door (Al-Bab al-Maftouh) by Latifa al-Zayyat (1960)

A landmark of women's writing in Arabic, the novel explores a middle-class Egyptian girl's coming of age, both sexually and politically, during the growing Egyptian nationalist movement of the 1940s and 50s against the British-established monarchy, the 1952 revolution and the 1956 Suez Canal nationalisation. An animated and modern portrayal of Layla and her brother's struggle to free themselves from family and social constrictions of the time, it is noted for its bold use of colloquial Arabic and spirited dialogue.

Latifa al-Zayyat (1923–1996) was born in Damietta, Egypt, and studied for her BA and PhD in English Literature at Cairo University. She became professor of English at the Girls College, Ain Shams University, Cairo, later chair of the department of English, and director of the Egyptian Arts Academy. *The Open Door* was adapted to film in 1963, and was awarded the inaugural Naguib Mahfouz Medal for Literature in 1996.

38 Sultana by Ghalib Halasa (1988)

Sultana is Ghalib Halasa's multi-layered and semi-autobiographical masterpiece, delving into the social and political tensions which pervaded Jordan during the mid-twentieth century through numerous characters, stories and dialects. At the centre of this web is Sultana: an extraordinary woman who relies on no one, and through whose eventful life Halasa skilfully weaves together the modern history of Jordan.

Ghalib Halasa (1932–1989) was born in Ma'in, Jordan. He received a BA in Journalism from the American University of Beirut and went on to live in Baghdad, Cairo and Damascus, permanently exiled from Jordan for his Communist beliefs. During his lifetime he wrote seven novels and two collections of short stories, considered among the best of modern Arab literature, and contributed regularly to newspapers.

39 Maryam: Keeper of Stories (Maryam al-Hakayah) by Alawiya Sobh (2002)

Set during the Lebanese Civil War, this novel is a refreshing depiction of different women's experiences during a turbulent period in Middle Eastern history. At the centre of this cluster of diverse and yet intertwined accounts is Maryam who, fearful of the erasure of memories left untold, zealously takes over the role of storyteller from her friend and would-be narrator Alawiya. Through tales of love, passion, pain and transformation, this novel intimately reflects on the art of preserving and reviving memories, even from the darkest points in our lives.

Alawiya Sobh (b.1955) is a Lebanese novelist, short-story writer and journalist. In the early 1990s, she founded *Snob al-Hasnaa'*, a

widely-read women's magazine. She has been guest speaker on television programmes concerning women, war and modernity in Lebanon. *Maryam al-Hakayah*, for which Sobh was awarded the 2006 Sultan Qabbous Prize, was acclaimed as a novel of epic dimensions and was widely reviewed in the Arab world.

40 Haddatha Abu Huraira Qal
(Thus Spoke Abu Huraira) by Mahmoud Messadi (1939)

This is the riveting tale of Abu Huraira, a man whose scrupulous and devout lifestyle is thrown into jeopardy by the appearance of an old friend who urges him to leave the confines of Mecca and explore the world at large. As they set out together to the desert, so begins Abu Huraira's journey of self-discovery: unable to maintain his previous convictions, his wanderings are increasingly motivated by his quest to find the truth, to find God and, ultimately, to find himself.

Mahmoud Messadi (1911–2004), born in Tazerka in the coastal governorate of Nabeul, Tunisia, is lauded as one of the most important Tunisian authors and intellectuals. He studied Arabic and French Literature at the Sorbonne, Paris, and after Independence, became Secretary of State of National Education, 1958 to 1968. He helped to set up the post-Independence modern, bilingual and nationwide education system. He was Minister of Cultural Affairs 1973 to 1976. His complete works were published by the Tunisian state in 1994.

41 Death in Beirut (Tawahin Bayrut [Windmills of Beirut]) by Tawfiq Yusuf Awwad (1972)

In the fragile political climate of post-1967 Lebanon, a young woman called Tamina defies the wishes of her family and community by leaving her small Shia Muslim village to study in Beirut. This bold move acquires even greater significance when she arrives there and makes two life-changing acquaintances: Hani, a Maronite Christian student activist and Ramzi, a revolutionary journalist and poet. As her own political activism intensifies and her relationship with these two men blossoms, she is lured towards a dramatic climax which foreshadows the horrific events in Lebanon of 1975.

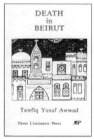

Tawfiq Yusuf Awwad (1911–1989) was a Lebanese author and diplomat. He was born in the village of Bhersaf in Mount Lebanon, where he was educated before enrolling in the Jesuit College of St. Joseph in Beirut. He initially became a journalist, writing for the Lebanese newspaper *An-Nahar*, however in 1946 he joined the diplomatic service and was subsequently posted to Europe, Asia and South America. His monumental novel *Al-Raghif* (1939; The Loaf) sealed his reputation as one of the great figures of modern Arabic literature.

42 The Hostage (Al-Rahina) by Zayd Mutee' Dammaj (1984)

Set during the lead up to Yemen's brief revolution of 1948, this acclaimed novel revolves around the trials and tribulations of a young boy taken from his family by the Imamate to secure his father's political obedience. Sent to work as a servant in the Governor's palace, he is quickly overwhelmed by its toxic atmosphere, where relationships are fuelled by sex and power, and the situation is further exacerbated by the rumblings of political dissidence outside the palace walls. A gripping read, this is as much a reflection on loss of innocence as it is on this important moment in Yemen's modern history.

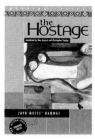

Zayd Mutee' Dammaj (1943–2000), novelist and short story writer, was born in As Sayyani District, Ibb Governorate, Yemen. He was educated in his hometown and then in Egypt before enrolling in law and, subsequently, journalism at Cairo University. His literary career had already begun when his father summoned him to Yemen in 1968 to participate in the revolutionary movement. In 1970 he was elected to the Shura Council, Yemen's first elected parliament, and later served as ambassador to Kuwait. Throughout his political career he continued to write fiction, earning great acclaim for his debut novel *The Hostage*.

43 Al-Laz (The Ace) by Tahar Wattar (1974)

In this gripping novel of the Algerian revolution, events revolve around Al-Laz, a young man who seeks to deflect from the shame of his illegitimate birth by joining the struggle for independence. However, after finally discovering his father Zaydan, a Communist who runs a guerrilla cell in the mountains, he is faced with the horrific reality that his father will be executed by his own countrymen for refusing to recant his political beliefs. Wattar exposes both the heroic sacrifices made and the darker aspect of internal ideological conflicts which marked this bloody episode in Algerian history.

Tahar Wattar (1936–2010) has been described as the father of the Algerian novel. Born in Sedrata in Souk Ahras Province into a Berber family, he received an education in Islamic jurisprudence before turning to literature. He began working as a journalist in the early sixties, after Independence. However, after publishing his first collection of short stories in Arabic in 1965, he became a prolific novelist. The English translation of his novel *The Earthquake* came out in 2000. In 2005 he was awarded the Sharjah Prize for Arab Culture, and in 2009 the Owais Prize.

44 In Praise of Hatred (Madih al-Karahiya) by Khaled al-Khalifa (2006)

This novel documents a society under the double repression of the Muslim Brotherhood and the Syrian Ba'ath Party, as well as the battle for power between them in the 1970s, culminating in the massacre of Hama (1982). The narrating voice is that of a female fundamentalist. Hatred, the author suggests, is a propelling force just like love. The novel was first published in Damascus in 2006, but later banned by the Syrian government before being re-published in Lebanon. The novel's English translation was longlisted for the 2013 Independent Foreign Fiction Prize.

Khaled Khalifa, born in 1964 in Aleppo, Syria, with a degree from Aleppo University in law, is a novelist, poet, and screenwriter for television dramas, documentaries and short films. He lives in Damascus and has written five novels. *In Praise of Hatred* was shortlisted for the inaugural International Prize for Arabic Fiction (IPAF) in 2008. His next, *No Knives in the Kitchens of This City* (2013), won the Naguib Mahfouz Medal for Literature and was shortlisted for the 2014 IPAF. Most of his work focuses on the pain inflicted on the Syrian people by despotism and fundamentalism.

45 Najmat Aghustus (August Star) by Sonallah Ibrahim (1974)

This novel was initially published in Damascus and banned in Egypt. A journalist travels to Upper Egypt to investigate the deaths of Egyptian workers and the environmental damage caused in the initial stages of the construction of the Aswan High Dam. Finding little to record, the journalist supplements his field research with articles from newspapers and magazines, which depict a situation far rosier than the real one. The enterprise highlights the irony of the co-operation between the Soviet Union and an Egyptian government that imprisons Egyptian communists. The Dam emerges as a symbol of progress and injustice at the same time.

46 Memory in the Flesh (Dhakirat al-Jasad) by Ahlam Mosteghanemi (1993)

Spread over the turbulent period of Algeria's history from the 1940s to the 1980s, this is the story of Khaled, a middle-aged militant who lost his arm during the War of Independence and is now a famous painter in Paris. Stirred by his unlikely and complicated love affair with Hayat, a novelist many years his junior and the daughter of Si Taher, a freedom fighter and his old friend, he is drawn into his memories – both fond and painful – of the homeland he has not visited for decades. A compelling insight into the social and political history of postcolonial Algeria, framed by a passionate love story.

Ahlam Mosteghanemi is an Algerian author, born in Tunis in 1953, where her family had moved to after her father, a prominent Algerian nationalist, was released from prison. After Independence in 1962, her family returned to Algeria, where she attended one of the first Arabic-language schools, and later completed her PhD at the Sorbonne. Since then she has published several collections of poetry and novels. In 1998 she was awarded the Naguib Mahfouz Medal for Literature.

47 The Bamboo Stalk (Saaq al-Bambou) by Saud Alsanousi (2012)

This unusual coming-of-age story examines problems of race, religion and identity through the life of a half-Filipino, half-Kuwaiti

young man Jose/Isa, who moves from an impov-
erished life in the Philippines to return to his father's Kuwait to explore his origins – a 'paradise',
as his Filipina mother has described it to him since
he was a child. There he eventually discovers that
he doesn't belong in either country. This daring
novel approaches the highly charged and emo-
tional subject of Kuwaiti social dynamics in ways
that are both sensitive and measured.

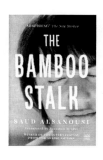

Saud Alsanousi (b.1981) is a Kuwaiti novelist
and journalist. His debut novel, *The Prisoner of
Mirrors* (2010), won him the Leila Othman
Prize. His second, *The Bamboo Stalk* (2012),
won the 2013 IPAF. In 2011 his short story, *The
Bonsai and the Old Man*, won the 'Stories on the
Air' competition organised by *Al-Arabi* maga-
zine and BBC Arabic. His third novel, *Mama
Hissa's Mice* (2015) is being translated.

48 Urs Baghl (A Mule's Wedding) by Tahar Wattar (1978)

Wattar seamlessly blends perceptions of reality
and fantasy in this intimate glimpse into Algeria's
underworld. A devout sheikh named Kiyan, determined that even the city's brothels should benefit from his religious inspiration, finds himself
falling in love with a well-known brothel owner
and singer, Inabiya. An engaging tale which explores the depths of human desire and the pull towards escapism, whilst critically observing the many social issues
which prevailed in postcolonial Algeria.

49 Midaq Alley (Zuqaq al-Madaq) by Naguib Mahfouz (1966)

Midaq Alley is a cross section of a bustling back
alley in Cairo, inhabited by an array of characters:
Zaita, the cripple-maker, Kirsha, a café owner

who likes boys and drugs, Umm Hamida, the marriage broker and her ambitious daughter Hamida who dreams of reaching a higher status through marriage. Mahfouz describes his characters with subtle irony, whilst denouncing a society too prone towards everything Western and material gains and reluctant to appreciate traditional values. *Midaq Alley* was adapted for the cinema twice, in 1963 under the direction of Hassan al-Imam and in 1995 with a film set in Mexico City, directed by Jorge Fons.

50 My Name is Adam. Children of the Ghetto (Ismi Adam. Awlad el-Gheto) by Elias Khoury (2016)

This first volume of a trilogy tells the story of Palestinian Adam Dannoun and his attempt to write a novel after emigrating to New York. When he meets blind Ma'moun, a father figure from his childhood, he begins to find out the truth of his own identity and reconnect with his memories of Lydda, Palestine, where in 1948 the city fell, many of its people massacred by the Israeli occupying forces who forced an exodus of almost all the rest of its inhabitants. Adam's mother was one who remained, with baby Adam, the first child of the ghetto. His story is how those left, corralled into a ghetto fenced by barbed wire, coped with living, the loss, the silence, the memories, the ferocious unreality of their new life.

51 The Fetishists (Al-Majus) by Ibrahim al-Koni (1990)

This epic novel, considered the author's masterpiece, opens with the arrival of a mysterious caravan at a valley of the Sahara. With it come scorching winds from the south as well as gold, slaves, ancient tales and black magic. There the caravan wants to settle and build a city. Sultan Oragh of Timbuktu, afraid of losing his daughter to the gods, sends her to hide with the Tuareg nomads, but clashes soon start between Sufis, and gold dust sellers, nomads and city dwellers, between those following Tuareg traditions and the Fetishists. A blend of folklore, history and adventure.

52 The Sinners (Al-Haram) by Yusuf Idris (1959)

In the gloomy early morning light on a sprawling agricultural estate in the Nile Delta, a man makes a shocking discovery: a baby's corpse, abandoned in the grounds. When it transpires that the new-born child was suffocated, the entire population of the estate is thrown into chaos – all minds are intent on bringing the killer, already blemished by the sinful conception of the child, to justice. As  the search for the suspect begins, however, it appears that the baby is one of many secrets that the estate has been hiding. In this captivating mystery, Idris offers profound insight into social values and class tension in pre-revolutionary rural Egypt.

 Yusuf Idris (1927–1991) is considered one of the great pioneers of modern Arabic literature. Born in the Egyptian village of Al Bayrum, he studied medicine at the University of Cairo and practised as a physician before he began writing fiction. His numerous short stories, plays and novels, often based on personal experience, are distinguished by their realistic portraits of everyday Egyptian life and speech. His novel *Qissat Hubb* (1956) was posthumously awarded the 1997 Naguib Mahfouz Medal for Literature and published in translation as *City of Love and Ashes* (1999).

53 Clamor of the Lake (Sakhab al-Buhaira) by Mohamed el-Bisatie (1994)

The murky waters of the omniscient lake are the setting which binds together these three intriguing tales. An old fisherman hears the moving life story of a woman and her two boys whom he befriends; a couple who scour the shores of the lake for objects to sell stumble across a chest which speaks an incomprehensible language; and two neighbours develop an unlikely bond when their

businesses are jeopardized by the mysterious lake-dwellers. Yet amidst these curious incidents, no one can anticipate just how inextricably linked their fates have become to the whims of the lake .

Mohamed el-Bisatie (1937–2012) was an Egyptian novelist and short story writer. Born in el-Gamalia in the Nile Delta, he graduated from Cairo University in 1960 and embarked on a career as a civil servant. He first began writing fiction in the early sixties, publishing short stories in prestigious literary journals such as *Al Majalla*. He went on to write seven volumes of short stories and eleven novels.

54 Call of the Curlew (Du'a al-Karawan) by Taha Hussein (1934)

A tragic tale which explores themes of love, betrayal and social convention, set in early twentieth-century Upper Egypt. Amna is the bold and spirited narrator: a young woman from a village called Beni Warkan, tainted by her late father's licentious behaviour and forced to move with her mother and sister to the city. However, when a romantic liaison with a wealthy young engineer

results in her sister's murder, an outraged Amna resolves to take justice into her own hands and avenge her death. Adapted for film in 1959, it is considered a classic of Egyptian cinema.

Taha Hussein (1889–1973) was a pioneer of the modernist movement in Egyptian literature. Born in Minya Governorate in Upper Egypt, a mistreated eye infection led to him becoming blind at three years old. He initially studied at Al-Azhar University, later gaining a doctorate from Cairo University and then the Sorbonne. When he returned from France he became a professor of Arabic literature at Cairo University, and later served as Minister of Education. A prolific novelist and essayist, he is probably best known for his internationally acclaimed memoir *The Days* (*Al-Ayyam*, 1933).

55   Ana Ahya (I Live) by Layla Baalbaki (1958)

A novel which was so controversial as to effect a political uproar, this is the account of the innermost thoughts and emotions of Lina, a courageous young Lebanese woman who rejects society's expectations of her role as a female. Through Lina's struggle for social, political and financial independence, Baalbaki candidly examines the inherent difficulties and repercussions of individually challenging the prevailing social culture.

Layla Baalbaki is a Lebanese author, journalist and activist, born in southern Lebanon in 1936. She studied literature at Saint Joseph University in Beirut, however she left before graduating to work as a secretary in the Lebanese parliament. She published her first novel, *Ana Ahya*, at the age of 22, following this with a short story collection in 1963. The controversial and sexually explicit content of both works landed her in court on charges of obscenity and harming public morality. Although her name was eventually cleared, she subsequently stopped writing works of fiction and focused on her career as a journalist.

56   The Last of the Angels (Akhir al-Mala'ika) by Fadhil al-Azzawi (1992)

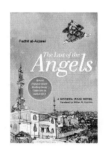

Set in 1950s Kirkuk, Iraq, al-Azzawi's acclaimed novel merges the comical and the fantastical with modern Iraqi history. The novel follows the lives of three young men from one neighbourhood: Hameed Nylon, the chauffeur-turned-revolutionary; Khidir Musa, who travels to the Soviet Union in search of his long lost brothers and Burhan Abdullah, who uncovers an old chest in his attic which allows him to communicate with angels. Through their distinct and often bizarre stories, al-Azzawi paints a vivid and moving scene of northern Iraqi society in the years preceding the overthrow of the monarchy.

Fadhil al-Azzawi was born in Kirkuk, northern Iraq, in 1940. He has a BA in English Literature from Baghdad University and a PhD in Journalism from Leipzig University. He edited literary magazines and newspapers in Iraq and abroad and has been publishing poetry since the 1960s, founding the poetry magazine *Shi'r 69*. He left Iraq in 1977 to settle in Germany, and has translated several German literary works into Arabic.

57 The Lodging House (Wikalat Atiya) by Khairy Shalaby (1999)

A young man hides in a rundown caravanserai after assaulting his teacher who discriminated against him. He comes across a range of characters living at the margins of society whose stories of joy and sorrow create an almost magical world that echoes traditional Arab storytelling. The narrating voice only manages to appear spasmodically, as one of the characters takes over the narration. In 2003, the novel won the Naguib Mahfouz Medal for Literature and in 2007 Farouk Abdul Wahab's English translation won the Saif Ghobash Banipal Translation Prize.

Khairy Shalaby (1938–2011) was a prolific Egyptian novelist, short-story writer and literary critic. In 1980-81 he was awarded the Egyptian National Prize for Literature. He was editor-in-chief of *Poetry Magazine* and the Library of Popular Studies, published by the Egyptian Ministry of Culture. Shalaby wanted to be the voice of the Egyptian people.

58 Mawt Saghir (Small Death)
by Mohammed Hasan Alwan (2016)

This fictional account of the life of twelfth-century Sufi scholar, poet and philosopher Ibn Arabi follows his travels from Andalusia to Damascus, as well as his inner turmoil searching for the meaning of life and love. Written in the style of a medieval travelogue, Ibn Arabi reports on his encounters, on the experience of violence witnessed along his journey, his life as a man with feelings and foibles, showing him in many ways as a contemporary figure. The novel won the 2017 IPAF prize, the judges noting its striking artistry and captivating language.

Mohammed Hasan Alwan is an IT engineer and a writer of novels and short stories from Saudi Arabia, born in Riyadh in 1979, and now based in Canada. His work was included in Beirut39, an anthology featuring the 39 best Arab authors under the age of 40, in the collection *Emerging Arab Voices*, *Banipal*, *The Guardian* and *Words Without Borders*. His novel *al-Qundus* (2011, The Beaver) was shortlisted for the 2013 IPAF and won the Institut du monde arabe's 2015 Prix de la Litterature Arabe.

59 The Committee (Al-Lajna)
by Sonallah Ibrahim (1981)

The nameless narrator is summoned before a mysterious Committee of Investigation to answer questions on a topic about which he has received no firm information. The series of hearings progresses in a way that has often been described as "Kafkaesque". Asked to suggest what the present century will most be remembered for, for example, he eventually ventures the answer "Coca-Cola". Later, when the Committee informs him that he is to prepare a study of the most prominent contemporary Arab personality, he chooses a cryptically named "Doctor", but the choice does not meet with the Committee's approval. When his efforts to satisfy the Committee all fail, he is sentenced to the harshest punishment available to the Committee – to eat himself.

60 The Seven Days of Man (Ayyam al-Insan al-Sab'ah) by Abdel Hakim Qasem (1969)

Set in a small village in the Nile Delta region, this story traces the annual pilgrimage of a group of dervishes to the Sufi shrine of Al-Sayyid Al-Badawi. Spread across a period of fifteen years, the son of the group leader, Abdel Aziz, relates each of the seven ceremonial stages of this pilgrimage with a particular stage in his life. Yet, as time progresses and his understanding of the world beyond the confines of the village develops, we observe the drastic changes in Abdel Aziz's attitude towards the rituals he so vividly describes, epitomizing the inevitable crisis of a life torn between tradition and modernity.

Abdel Hakim Qasem (1934–1990) was born in the village of El Bandara in Gharbia Governorate, Egypt, moving to Cairo in the 1950s to begin his writing career. He was imprisoned for four years for his political views, after which he lived in exile in Berlin until 1985. He authored five novels, five short story collections, four novellas and a play. His work is renowned for its vivid depictions of the Egyptian countryside and Sufi traditions, which played a strong role in his early life.

61 Al-Diglah fi Arajiniha (Dates on their Branches) by Béchir Khraief (al-Bashir Khurayyif) (1969)

Set in the early twentieth century in Djerid, a remote semi-desert region in southwestern Tunisia, the novel revolves around the every-

day struggles faced by a family of ancient de-
scent whose livelihood depends on the region's
plentiful date palms. Yet as years pass by and
both the family and community are torn apart
by land disputes, poverty, love and jealousy, a
vivid picture emerges of the many conflicts and
hardships which afflicted Tunisian society as a
result of the French colonial presence.

Béchir Khraief (Al-Bashir Khurayyif)
(1917–1983) was a Tunisian novelist and
short story writer born in Nefta, Tozeur
Governorate. He received a religious education in his early years and worked in
trading wool and silk. However, he later
switched professions to teaching. In the
late 1950s, he began publishing works of
fiction in the Tunisian literary magazine
al-Fikr, alongside the works of his brother, the famous poet
Mustapha Khraief. Regarded as a pioneer of the Tunisian novel, Khurayyif shocked many with the unprecedented use of colloquial
Tunisian in his works.

62   Al-Masarrat wal-Awja' (Joys and Pains)
by Fuad al-Takarli (1998)

Spanning from the early 20th century to the
dawn of the Iran-Iraq War in 1980, this is the
story of Tawfiq, the son of a traditional Iraqi family from the city of Khanaqin. Although he
spends his early years in comfort and content-
ment, his life as a young adult soon begins to di-
verge drastically from the experiences and
expectations of his family. As Tawfiq falls increasingly into a debauched lifestyle, drifting between

pleasure and anguish – both his own and others – the novel is a stark
and fascinating reflection on the human propensity to strive for personal fulfilment, at any cost.

63 The Stone of Laughter (Hajar al-Dhihk) by Hoda Barakat (1990)

The novel, set in the Lebanese Civil War, features, for the first time in the history of Arabic fiction, a homosexual protagonist, Khalil. After losing the two men he loves in the war, Khalil isolates himself and becomes ill. The job at a magazine doesn't seem to help him heal. After being operated on for an ulcer, he decides to forget Naji, his first love, by renting his flat out. From this point onwards, Khalil's humanity gradually dissolves, his heart hardens: he becomes a drug and arms dealer and a rapist.

Hoda Barakat (b.1952) is a Lebanese author who lived through the Lebanese Civil War. During that time she worked as a journalist, and a teacher. In 1989 she moved to Paris where she worked as a radio broadcaster. She has won many awards, including the 2001 Naguib Mahfouz Medal for Literature for her third novel *The Tiller of Waters* and the 2017-18 Al-Owais Award for the Novel. In 2002 she was honoured as Chevalier of the Order of Arts and Letters by the French Minister of Culture, and in 2015 shortlisted for the International Man Booker Prize. Most of her work focuses on war and trauma.

64 The Dove's Necklace (Tawq al-Hamam) by Raja Alem (2010)

The main narrator is neither the author nor one of her human characters, but a neighbourhood in Mecca, "Abu Alroos" (the Many-Headed), where most of her characters dwell. When human characters begin telling the story, it becomes revelation rather than narration. The novel is a journey across time and space, an attempt to break material barriers by creating virtual or spiritual spaces, sometimes intellectual ones. Characters are surrounded by walls and their lives dominated by legends, harsh societal restrictions and the economic system and its powers. Some choose to stay where fate has placed them, others decide to break free in a journey towards the freedom of the soul and its unlimited creative powers.

Raja Alem is a novelist from Saudi Arabia. She began publishing her work in the cultural supplement of *Al-Riyadh* newspaper and writing experimental plays for the theatre, short stories and novels. She has won many prizes, including the Arab Women's Creative Writing Prize on the 60th anniversary of the founding of UNESCO, the Lebanese Literary Club Prize in 2008. *The Dove's Necklace* was joint winner of the 2011 IPAF.

65   Dear Mr Kawabata (Azizi al-Sayyed Kawabata) by Rashid al-Daif (1995)

In the final days of the Lebanese Civil War, a mortally wounded revolutionary named Rashid surveys his life, intriguingly addressing his memoir to the deceased Japanese novelist Yasunari Kawabata. Between bouts of consciousness, Rashid's thoughts and memories are shaped into an extraordinary discourse in which he ponders intellectual and existential questions, simultaneously 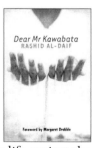 recounting the personal struggles he has faced in his life against the backdrop of this turbulent moment in Lebanese history.

Rashid al-Daif was born in Ehden, Lebanon, in 1945. He studied Arabic literature at the Lebanese University in Beirut and went on to complete two doctorates in Paris. Since 1974, he has been lecturing in Arabic literature at the American University of Beirut and the Lebanese University. A prolific novelist he is considered a vibrant and innovative voice in modern Arabic fiction. His novel *Dear Mr Kawabata* has been translated into a number of European languages.

66 Cairo Swan Song (Taghridat al-Baj'aa) by Mekkawi Said (2007)

Set in the late Seventies, this is the testimony of a generation of Egyptian intellectuals trying to come to terms with a difficult historical transition. Mustafa, the protagonist, is a left-wing figure who seems to be always on the wrong side, whether it be politically, socially or even in his relationships with women. He observes Cairo as the city collapses in a deep abyss, and feels alienated, whilst his once leftist friends have become capitalists or Islamists. The novel was shortlisted for IPAF in 2008 and won the Egyptian State Prize for Literature. It was translated in English by Adam Talib and published by AUC Press in 2009.

Mekkawi Said (1956–2017) was an Egyptian script writer, publisher, short-story writer and novelist. He published his first collection of short stories, *Running Towards the Light*, in 1981. Since then, he has published many novels, as well as writing scripts for short and long movies and documentaries. He also wrote for children's magazines throughout the Arab world. He was awarded the Suad Sabbah Arab Creativity Prize in 1991.

67 The Days (Al-Ayyam, 3 volumes) by Taha Hussein (1929 & 1973)

Taha Hussein's masterpiece three-part autobiography is a striking account of his early life. Beginning in a small village in Upper Egypt, we accompany him through his difficult childhood as he comes to terms with his blindness, a struggle over which he ultimately triumphs by winning a place at the prestigious Al-Azhar University. Through his experiences as a student in Cairo we witness the formation of an astonishing intellect, and an insatiable desire for knowledge which leads him to undertake a doctorate at the Sorbonne. Touching, humorous and utterly unreserved, this is primarily a tale of strength and perseverance in the face of constant challenge.

68 Al-Waba' (The Epidemic) by Hani al-Rahib (1981)

Hani al-Rahib's landmark fourth novel surveys the tragic history of a beleaguered people through a hundred years of modern Syrian history – from 1870 through two world wars, spanning three generations, the last of which finds itself in prison. It is a novel of horror and terror, rich and complex in character relations and events, leaving many questions unanswered. It brings to light the rise of the middle class in the Arab world – proponents of social justice who ultimately focused on their own political gains and abandoned the masses. The novel became a bible for Syrian political prisoners: when the author was presented with a torn prison copy, it contained more than a hundred signatures and commentaries, including notes from former military officer, General Salah Jadid. It is itself the modern history of Syria. Nothing else like it exists.

Hani al-Rahib (1939–2000) was born in Mashqitah, a suburb of the Syrian coastal city Latakia, to a religious Muslim family, and over 40 years wrote seven novels, all notable for their themes of protest, rebellion and rejection, all till now untranslated into English except for an excerpt from *The Epidemic* in *Banipal 9* after he died. While still a student at Damascus University, in 1961 he published his first novel, *Al-Mahzumun* [The Defeated], receiving an award from *Al-Adab* magazine. He spent his life in search of an Arab awakening, as an Arab man working to create a new society in the Arab world and a new culture. In so doing he broke taboos and explored forbidden themes. He was defeated by the same society that he long wished to change though he never failed to expose its fundamental weakness, corruption and absence of social justice.

69   Najran taht al-Sifr (Najran Below Zero) by Yahya Yakhlif (1975)

Banned throughout most of the Arab world, this novel is a powerful depiction of the devastation wrought by the North Yemen Civil War on the population of Najran, a border region in Saudi Arabia. Focussing in particular on the desperate poverty and repression of Arab migrant workers there, it follows the life of Abu Shannan, who, recently released from prison, becomes embroiled in the politics of the conflict. Yakhlif strikingly examines the dangerous consequences of religious fundamentalism and foreign intervention through the lens of this turbulent period in modern Arab history.

Yahya Yakhlif is a Palestinian novelist and writer. Born in Samakh in 1944, he and his family were displaced four years after his birth, leading to him living in countries such as Syria and Saudi Arabia. He has authored several short story collections and three novels, of which *A Lake beyond the Wind* (Buhayrah wara' al-Rih) was translated to English in 1998.

70   Miramar by Naguib Mahfouz (1967)

Set in 1960s Alexandria at a small hotel on the seafront, the Miramar, this novel is centred on the intersecting lives of a group of its guests. The overwhelming focus of their attention is Zohra, a beautiful young peasant girl who fled village life and now works at the hotel. Yet, as the guests contend for Zohra's affection and loyalty, events quickly spiral out of control, shedding light not only on the volatility of human emotion, but also the dramatic social and political changes of post-revolutionary Egypt which each character must come to terms with.

71 Beirut Nightmares (Kawabis Bayrut) by Ghada Samman (1976)

Caught in the turmoil of the Lebanese Civil War, a journalist is confined to her apartment in Beirut for two weeks during an intensive bombardment. Driven to the point of delirium by her imprisonment, she composes a series of episodes or "nightmares", which range between hallucinations, real nightmares and renditions of the horrific reality around her. Featuring an extraordinary array of characters, these nightmares reflect not only on the social issues which prompted the civil war, but also the extremities to which human beings can be pushed before reality and fantasy become indistinguishable.

Ghada al-Samman is a Syrian novelist, journalist and short story writer, and one of the most prominent female authors of the Arab world. Born in Damascus in 1942, she graduated in English literature from the Syrian University in 1963 and moved to Beirut to undertake an MA in theatre. She published her first collection of short stories in 1962, but after she began working as a journalist in Beirut she started writing fiction prolifically, even establishing her own publishing house. Her widely acclaimed work often addresses feminist and political issues in the Arab world.

72 The American Granddaughter (Al-Hafida al-Amerikiya) by Inaam Kachachi (2008)

The American occupation of Iraq is seen through the eyes of a young American-Iraqi woman, who returns to her country as an interpreter for the US Army. Through the narrator's conflicting emotions, we see the tragedy of a country which, having battled to emerge from dictatorship, then finds itself under foreign occupation.

Inaam Kachachi was born in Baghdad in 1952, and studied journalism at Baghdad University, working in Iraqi press and radio before moving to Paris to complete a PhD at the Sorbonne. She is the Paris correspondent for London-based newspaper *Asharq Al-Awsat* and *Kol Al-Usra* magazine in Sharjah, UAE. Kachachi's works include IPAF shortlisted *The American Granddaughter* and *Lorna*, a biography of British journalist Lorna Hales, who was the wife of pioneer Iraqi sculptor Jawad Salim. She produced and directed a documentary on Naziha Al Dulaimi, the first woman to become minister of an Arab country, in 1959.

73 Al-Raghif (Bread) by Tawfiq Yusuf Awwad (1939)

This was one of the first Arabic novels to explore the devastating effects of the First World War on the Arab region. The setting is Mount Lebanon in 1916, when Arab resistance to the Ottoman occupation is as ferocious as the famine which rages across the area, claiming thousands of lives. The narrative is centred on Sami Asim, a nationalist militant who is on the run from the Ottoman forces, and his beloved Zeina, who will go to any lengths to save him. A profound and often shocking insight into a previously untold story of human suffering, which saw the book hailed as a literary triumph.

74 The President's Gardens (Hadai'q al-Ra'is) by Muhsin al-Ramli (2012)

Set during the last fifty years of Iraqi history, the novel tells the story of three friends and explores how ordinary people have been affected by wars, the sanctions against Iraq and the invasion of Kuwait. It examines the gap between the lifestyle of those in power and ordinary citizens. During the chaos of occupation, one of the three loses his life, like so many caught between loyalists of the old and new regimes. The gripping story of the complexities of successive tragedies besetting the "land between two rivers" is told with humanity, and life is somehow the victor despite all the obstacles.

Muhsin Al-Ramli is an Iraqi writer, poet, academic and translator, born in the village of Sudara in northern Iraq in 1967. He has lived in Madrid since 1995 and received a PhD in literature and philosophy from Madrid University. He published his first work in 1985 and writes in both Arabic and Spanish. Over the years he has worked as a journalist and cultural editor for the Arab, Spanish and Latin American press and has translated a number of literary works from Arabic into Spanish and vice versa. He has published more than 20 books, ranging from short stories to plays, translations and novels. His novel *Dates on my Fingers* was longlisted for the 2010 IPAF and published in English translation in 2014.

75 The Arch and the Butterfly (Al-Qaws wal-Farasha) by Mohammed Achaari (2010)

The novel concerns the life of a left-wing Moroccan writer, Yousef, whose past life, political beliefs and faith in his own principles are shaken by a letter he receives one day. His young son, Yassin, raised in a secular family on principles of open-mindedness and free thinking, and who was sent to a prestigious Paris academy to study architecture, has chosen an opposite route to that which he had been prepared for. The anonymous

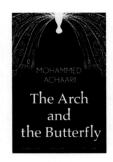

letter tells his father that the son "died as a martyr in Afghanistan". In following Yousef's steps re-assessing his past life, the author explores the story of a generation of Arab left-wing activists who all faced the same dilemmas and spent years of their youth behind bars and long hours in passionate debates, building a dream of a better life, only to end up in frustration and bitterness.

Mohammed Achaari was born in 1951 in Zerhoun, Morocco. After studying Law and Administration, he worked in political and cultural journalism and was editor of a number of newspapers and cultural supplements. He has written articles on literature and the arts alongside poetry and short stories. For three consecutive years, he was head of the Union of Moroccan writers and his political work led him to take up various government posts, including that of Minister of Culture in Morocco between 1998 and 2007. His eleven poetry collections have been published in Baghdad, Beirut and Casablanca, and he is regarded as one of the most prominent poetic voices of the 1970s generation in Morocco. *The Arch and the Butterfly* jointly won the 2011 IPAF and was nominated for the Italian Ziator Prize.

76 The Vagrant (Sharid al-Manazil) by Jabbour Douaihy (2010)

The Vagrant provides a realistic, engaging portrayal of the Lebanese civil war through the eyes of a young man, Nizam, who finds himself uprooted by the conflict. The hero represents the crisis of the Lebanese individual imposed upon by a sectarian reality. The novel follows his struggle to belong as he faces unfamiliar situations and conflicts in a society that considers him an outsider.

Jabbour Douaihy was born in Zgharta, northern Lebanon, in 1949. He holds a PhD degree in Comparative Literature from the Sorbonne and works as Professor of French Literature at the University of Lebanon. To date, he has published seven works of fiction, including novels, short stories and children's books. His novel *June Rain* was shortlisted for the inaugural IPAF in 2008 and published in English by Bloomsbury Qatar Foundation Publishing in July 2014. *The Vagrant* was shortlisted for the IPAF prize in 2012.

77 Al-Ashjar wa-Ightiyal Marzouq (The Trees and the Assassination of Marzouq) by Abdelrahman Munif (1973)

A young history lecturer, dismissed from his position for not teaching the 'standard' version of modern Arab history, is forced to leave his homeland and take a job in a neighbouring country as a French translator. However, as he embarks upon his journey there, he meets and learns the turbulent life story of the curious Ilyas, prompting a revival of disturbing memories of his own, of a life lived in constant fear where his only escape was into a world of fantasy and indulgence, the events which ultimately led to his miserable exile.

78 Aunt Safiyya and the Monastery (Khalti Safiyya wal-Deer) by Bahaa Taher (1991)

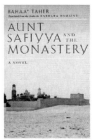

The author creates, through powerful and dramatic narrative, "a model community in a subtle and entertaining manner" in this novel set in Upper Egypt, where the author is from, and which has well-known customs of revenge killings and vendettas, as well as a centuries-old peaceful co-existence between Copts and Muslims. Taher famously focuses on these traditions that are in the full grip of modernising change through Haj, with his son, the narrator, confronting the blood-lust vengeance of Aunt Safiyya who demands the death of the man who killed her husband, and then joining forces with Coptic monk Bishai, who gave sanctuary to Harbi, the young man threatened with the blood vengeance.

79 The Theocrat (Majnoon al-Hukm) by Bensalem Himmich (1989)

The novel centres on the controversial figure of Fatimid Caliph al-Hakim bi-Amr Allah, who ruled Egypt from 996 to 1020. An unpredictable and suspicious ruler who fought to stay in power, but was also aware of his own psychological instability. As dissatisfaction spread amongst his people, his paranoia increased: Abu Rakwa would lead the revolt to dethrone him. After al-Hakim's demise some will remember him as a holy figure. *The Theocrat* won the al-Naqid Award, and the 1989 Riad el-Rayyes Prize.

Bensalem Himmich (b.1948) is a Moroccan novelist and poet. He writes in both Arabic and French and has published many novels, collections of poetry, works of philosophy and literary criticism. He was Minister of Culture of Morocco, 2009 to 2012. His novel *The Polymath*, inspired by Ibn Khaldun, was awarded the 2001 Naguib Mahfouz Medal for Literature and the 2003 Great Atlas Prize. His novel *Hadha Al-Andalusi!* was longlisted for the 2010 IPAF, with its English translation, under the title *A Muslim Suicide,* winning the 2012 Saif Ghobash Banipal Translation Prize. His novel *My Torturess* (2010) was shortlisted for the 2011 IPAF. Professor of Philosophy at the Mohammed V University in Rabat, Bensalem Himmich advocates the separation of religion and state, and has published extensively on the subject of ideology and Islam.

80 Adrift on the Nile (Thartharah fawqa al-Neel) by Naguib Mahfouz (1966)

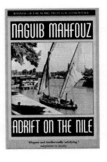

The book explores nihilism and spiritual emptiness, following protagonist Anis Zani who smokes kief every night with a group of friends on a houseboat on the Nile. Anis works as a civil servant and is disciplined for submitting a blank report – under the influence of drugs he didn't realize his pen had run out of ink. Soon a young journalist, Samara, visits them and the tranquillity of the group collapses as they begin to argue about love, morality, and purpose of life. The downfall of the group is accelerated when one night, as they are taking a midnight excursion by car, they hit a person and flee the scene. The novel was later adapted into the 1971 film Chitchat on the Nile.

81 Al-Mar'a wal-Warda (The Woman and the Rose) by Mohamed Zafzaf (1972)

A rare glimpse at the harsh reality of life in postcolonial Morocco, narrated through the eyes of a disillusioned intellectual who has failed to realize his grandiose dreams. Through the protagonist's eloquent, often surreal, reflections on relationships, power and social issues, the novel sheds a critical light on a country in which its thriving tourist industry seems to come at a price for its own citizens.

Mohamed Zafzaf (1945–2001) was one of Morocco's foremost modern authors and poets writing in Arabic. Born in Kantira, he studied philosophy at the Faculty des Letters and Human Sciences in Rabat, working as a teacher and a librarian before turning to writing. He published his first short story in 1963, after which he continued to write poetry, short story collections and novels, as well as to translate literature from Spanish and French into Arabic. One year after his death, the Mohamed Zafzaf Prize for Arabic Literature was established in his memory.

82 Diary of a Country Prosecutor (Yawmiyyat Nai'b fi al-Aryaf) by Tawfiq al-Hakim (1933)

This is the journal of a young prosecutor who investigates the homicide of Kamar al-Dawla Alwan. The only person who knows the facts is Reem, a good-looking adolescent who suddenly disappears without leaving any trace. The semi-autobiographical novel is a comedy of errors where the traditional setting of rural Egypt, described in cruel and comical terms, contrasts with the Western ideals the prosecutor has embraced during his studies abroad. The foreign,

"enlightened" legal system which he tries to impose on this destitute part of the world is difficult if not impossible to comprehend and apply.

83 The Longing of the Dervish (Shawq al-Darwish) by Hammour Ziada (2014)

The novel centres on the impossible love between Bakhit, a Muslim black slave, and Theodora, a white Christian who is murdered. Bakhit traces the possible murderers to six people against whom he will try and exact revenge. Set at the end of the nineteenth century, Sudan has experienced the overthrow of the Mahdist state. The novel touches upon the issue of slavery and freedom, faith and infidelity, the self and the other and is enriched with magical and superstitious anecdotes.

Hammour Ziada is a Sudanese writer, born in Khartoum in 1977. He wrote for a number of Sudanese publications such as *Al-Mustaqilla*, *Ajras al-Horriya*, and *Al-Jarida* and was cultural editor of *Al-Akhbar* daily newspaper there. He is author of several fiction works – novels *Al-Kunj* (2010) and *Longing of the Dervish* (2014) and two collections of short stories, *A Life Story from Omdurman* (2008) and *Sleeping at the Foot of the Mountain* (2014). *The Longing of the Dervish* won Hammour the 2014 Naguib Mahfouz Medal for Literature and was then longlisted for the 2015 IPAF.

84 Mukhmal (Velvet) by Huzama Habayeb (2016)

A harrowing and moving narrative of an ordinary young Palestinian woman living in a Jordanian refugee camp during the 1960s and 70s, doing her best to survive despite the harshness of the world around her, commuting back and forth between

the Baqaa Palestinian camp and her seamstress job in Amman. Her characters are "able to capture joy in the midst of oppression", the author explained last December when she was awarded the Naguib Mahfouz Medal for Literature. Her characters are real, fully dimensional people who feel passion and love, not allegorical symbols or heroes. The judges called it a "new kind of Palestinian novel".

Huzama Habayeb is a Palestinian author and journalist, born in Kuwait and graduating from Kuwait University in English language and literature. She worked there as a journalist until 1990 and the Gulf War, when she was forced to leave. In Jordan she established her reputation as a short story writer, publishing her first collection in 1992, rceiving prizes for her works in 1993 and 1994. In 2001 she published her fourth collection of short stories and in 2007 her first novel, *Root of Passion*, and two years later her first poetry collection. In 2011 came a second novel, while her third, entitled *Velvet*, was awarded the 2017 Naguib Mahfouz Medal for Literature. She lives in the UAE, where she works as a journalist for *Zahrat al-Khaleej* magazine, Abu Dhabi.

85 The Corpse Washer (Wahdaha Shajarat al-Rumman) by Sinan Antoon (2012)

This is the story of Jawad, a young Iraqi whose family prepares corpses for burial. Jawad insists on wanting to be a sculptor, against his father's wishes. But war is raging in Iraq, and with the American occupation, sectarianism increases and violence spreads. Jawad is forced to stop his studies and help his parents wash and shroud the corpses that are forever arriving, inadvertently

watering the lone pomegranate tree in the yard. He realizes that death shapes life and not vice versa, but the meticulous portrayal of the corpse-washing rituals, Jawad's ambivalent feelings about his work and the other world of his nightly dreams, show a gentler, more human side to the world of violence and brutality that is Iraq's complex and violent recent history.

Sinan Antoon, born in Baghdad in 1967, is a poet, novelist, scholar, journalist and literary translator now living in the US. He left Iraq in 1991, at the onset of the Gulf War. He is an associate professor at the Gallatin School, NY University. Antoon writes in both Arabic and English. His translations of poetry have won awards, as have his novels. *The Corpse Washer* was translated into English by Antoon himself, and won the 2014 Saif Ghobash Banipal Translation Prize, was long-listed for the 2014 Independent Foreign Fiction Prize. Its French edition won the 2017 Prix de la Littérature Arabe.

86 Disciples of Passion (Ahl al-Hawa) by Hoda Barakat (1993)

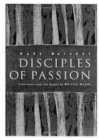

The story of an impossible love between a Christian man and a Muslim woman during the Lebanese Civil War as told by the unnamed man. After experiencing kidnap, hostage exchange and hospital internment, he becomes severely traumatised and starts questioning everything, even his own existence, while their relationship becomes increasingly fraught. His breakdown results in the killing of his lover. The story takes shape through his patchy first person narration, alternating between moments of confusion and clarity.

87 June Rain (Matar Huzairan) by Jabbour Douaihy (2006)

In June Rain Eliyya returns to his home town in the Lebanese mountains to learn the reasons that forced his family to migrate to the United States. Told from the perspective of different characters, the story documents the sectarian divisions caused by a massacre that happened in the village one June day in 1957, where Eliyya's father was shot dead. The narration weaves together childhood memories and the adult Eliyya's investigation.

88 The House of Mathilde (Binayat Matild) by Hassan Daoud (1983)

Hassan Daoud's debut novel is set in a building in Beirut during a war where people have managed to create an atmosphere of peaceful coexistence. The building is inhabited by a mysterious Russian family, an Armenian family, Muslims and Christians, and by the narrator's parents who come from the south. Life in the apartment block goes on normally and is dictated by daily routines, marriages, births and departures. These 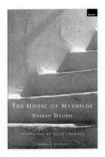 people survive, despite the war raging outside, but when violence breaks out in their building, everything changes.

 Hassan Daoud, born in Noumairieh in southern Lebanon in 1950, is a writer whose career as a journalist began with the outbreak of the Lebanese Civil War. He was a correspondent for *Al-Hayat* newspaper for 11 years and is currently editor of *Nawafez*, the cultural supplement of *Al-Mustaqbal* newspaper. He has written eight novels and two collections of short stories. In 2015 he was awarded the Naguib Medal for Literature for his novel *No Road to Paradise* (2013) and in 2010 his *180 Sunsets* was longlisted for the IPAF.

89 Return to Haifa ('Aid ila Haifa) by Ghassan Kanafani (1969)

Return to Haifa is considered one of the best novellas of modern Palestinian literature. It has been translated into many languages, among them Japanese, English, Russian and Persian. In the book, Ghassan Kanafani examines the concept of return and the concept of the home country. Said and his wife Safiyya return to their home in Haifa, which they had fled from twenty years earlier during the Nakba and when their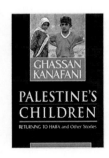

baby son Khaldun had been left behind. They are surprised to find that he is now a young man named Dov, a soldier in the Israeli Army, having been adopted by the Jewish family who occupied their home. The tragedy reaches its climax when the young man sides with his adoptive Jewish mother after learning the truth of his birth.

90 Al-Su'al (The Question) by Ghalib Halasa (1979)

Set in Egypt in the aftermath of the 1952 Revolution, *Al-Su'al* brings to life the hopes and preoccupations of this troubled period. Mustafa is a young intellectual whose Communist ideals alienate him from the social and political reality he experiences. His search for answers leads him to pursue illicit sexual encounters with women from lower social classes, one of whom is a married woman named Tafeeda — a relationship which will change both of their lives drastically . . .

91 Bab al-Saha (The Door to the Courtyard) by Sahar Khalifa (1990)

Set during the Palestinian first Intifada, in Nablus, the author's home town, this acclaimed novel confronts and lays bare the contradictory lives Palestinian women are forced to live day after day. All feisty characters, of different ages and with different experiences of life, in the close society where everyone knows everyone, the women reveal, through their conversations and actions, how they cope with the dichotomy of life meted out to them by traditional Palestinian society — on the one hand running families and becoming neighbourhood leaders when the menfolk are arrested, and on the other going along with the traditional role, being beaten by their brothers or husbands, forced to marry at a young age (not for love) and accepting society as it is. All the while, the Intifada rolls on in the background with young Hussam as token male, spending his time throwing stones at Israeli soldiers.

THE 100 BEST ARABIC NOVELS

Sahar Khalifeh, born in Nablus in 1941, Her writing focuses on Palestinians' daily life under occupation, and the discrimination against and oppression of Arab women. She has published 11 novels as well as many articles and studies. Many of her novels and other works have been translated into several languages, though *Bab al-Saha* has yet to appear in English. She has received many Arab and international awards, including the Naguib Mahfouz Medal for Literature, the Mohamed Zafzaf Prize for the Novel, the Simone de Beauvoir Prize (French readers' prize), the Alberto Moravia Award for International Fiction, and the Cervantes Prize for literature translated into Spanish.

92 Khamsat Aswat (Five Voices) by Ghaib Tu'ma Farman (1967)

Five Voices is probably Farman's best known novel. It describes and assesses the state of pre-1958 Iraqi society through five voices from Baghdad's middle-class: Said Ahmed, an ambitious journalist and writer; Ibrahim, a journalist who does his best to navigate a difficult political situation; Sherif, a bohemian poet who reminds people of the famous Iraqi poet Hussein Mardan; Abdelkhaliq, a graduate from the American University of Beirut who wants to reform society without being engaged with it; and finally Hameed, who lives a double life only Said Ahmed knows about.

93 The Bleeding of the Stone (Nazif al-Hajar) by Ibrahim al-Koni (1990)

The moufflon, a wild sheep prized for its meat, continues to survive in the remote mountain deserts of southern Libya. Only Asouf, a lone bedouin who cherishes the desert and identifies with its creatures, knows exactly where it is to be found. Now he and the moufflon together come under threat from hunters who have al-

ready slaughtered the once numerous desert gazelles. The novel combines pertinent ecological issues with a moving portrayal of traditional desert life and of the power of the human spirit to resist

94 Throwing Sparks (Tarmi bi-Sharar) by Abdo Khal (2010)

This dark novel follows the lives of three friends who grew up in the Firepit, a poor area of Jeddah. When they get taken on by a mysterious rich businessman in Jeddah, their lives are transformed. One, Tarek, who is also the narrator, becomes the hitman for his boss whose palace is the scene of sexual degradation, sadism, corruption and nightmares, where human evil is stretched to  the limit. The degenerate characters that populate the novel provide a bitter satire on a society that flaunts its purity and extreme wealth. The novel was banned in Saudi Arabia and several other Arab countries. It was awarded the 2010 IPAF prize.

 Abdo Khal, born in Al-Mijannah, Saudi Arabia, in 1962, is a journalist and the author of short stories, novels, poems and children's books, with a degree in Political Science from King Abdel Aziz University, Jeddah. He is editor-in-chief of the Saudi newspaper *Ukaz* and a board member of the Jeddah Literary Club. He is famous for using a mixture of classical Arabic and Hijazi dialect in his works as well as addressing the three arch taboos of sex, politics, and religion.

95 The Ship (Al-Safina) by Jabra Ibrahim Jabra (1970)

This acclaimed novel explores the Arab world after the Nakba of 1948 through a group of characters, alienated from their countries and isolated together on a ship at sea, which is cruising across the Mediterranean from Beirut to Naples. Two passengers, an Iraqi architect and a Palestinian businessman, act as narrators, the former having left Iraq to get away from a family feud, the latter yearning to be back in Palestine, having ended up in exile in Kuwait. Others, who know them, join the ship, and the beautifully written story unfolds, through dialogue and flashbacks, of tormented, interconnected and troubled relationships, of upheavals, of loss, of death, and of the human predicament of alienation and displacement from one's home. Published in English in 1985 by Three Continents Press.

96 Zahr al-Laymoun (Lemon Blossom) by Alaa al-Deeb (1987)

At the centre is the figure of Abdel Khalid al-Messiri, a divorced poet who works at a branch office of the Ministry of Culture in Suez, and who has suffered torture in prison and the consequences of the Infitah policy under Sadat. Messiri keeps returning to Cairo, a place he associates with painful events. And Cairo is the place where the neighbour's lemon tree used to be. What's left of it is the memory of a scent.

Al-Ahram newspaper described the novella as "one of the most remarkable novellas in the history of Arabic literature".

Alaa al-Deeb (1939–2016) was a journalist, short-story writer, screenwriter and translator of literary and political works into Arabic from English. He wrote a weekly literary column of book reviews "Assir al-Kutub" for over 40 years, first in *Sabah el-Kheir* magazine, then in *Al-Qahira* magazine and finally in *Al-Masri al-Youm*. In 2002 he was awarded the State Merit Award in Literature. *Banipal 60* dedicated its theme feature to his work, including an excerpt from *Lemon Blossom*. Otherwise his works are untranslated into English.

97 Qasr al-Matar (The Palace of Rain) by Mamdouh Azzam (1998)

Qasr al-Matar is the Syrian author's most celebrated and controversial novel. A powerful and daring treatment of taboos in the conservative Druze religion, the narrative plays out through the memories of Hassan, who has been reincarnated as Kamil al-Fadl. Remembering living a previous life as Kamil al-Fadl, and that he had been killed, the search begins through his memories for his killer. The story of the Al al-Fadl family, who have ended up living in abandoned ruins, comes to light, with Al al-Fadl struggling against both the tyranny of Kanj al-Hamdan and French Mandate colonialism. In examining the Great Syrian Revolt of 1925-27 against the French in the area of Jabal al-Arab/Jabal al-Druze, the novel caused great controversy among Druze society, whose elders claimed in a manifesto, which called for the death of the author (himself a Druze), that the novel harmed Druze society and their morals, sullied their tradition and customs, their taboos and legendary heroes. It asked for the book, published by the Syrian Ministry of Culture, to be banned.

Mamdouh Azzam was born in 1950 in al-Sweida, Syria, and has published six novels and a collection of stories, the first in 1985. His most celebrated work is the above novel *The Palace of Rain* (1998). His short novel *Ascension to Death* (Mi'raj al-Mawt), that was adapted for film in Syria, is the first of his works to be published in English translation (Haus Publishing, 2018).

98 Al-Washm (The Tattoo) by Abdul Rahman Majeed al-Rubaie (1972)

Protagonist Karim al-Nasiri is from the author's home town of Nasiriyah, south Iraq, where a good many of his compatriots are poor Shi'ites desperate for change. Karim appears to want to encourage this and becomes a member of a secret political party. But when he is imprisoned for his activities he decides to desert both the party and his comrades, and then leaves Nasiriyah for Baghdad. However, he finds no solution in the capital, and full of remorse for what he sees as his betrayal, ends up leaving Iraq too. *The Tattoo* is recognized as having an especially important place in the development of the Iraqi novel.

Abdul Rahman Majeed al-Rubaie is an Iraqi author and poet, born in the southern city of Nasiriyah in 1939. The themes and characters of his novels draw heavily on that southern countryside. His acclaimed debut novel, *Al-Washm*, excerpted in *Banipal 17*, was never published in Saddam's Iraq. He has more than 12 collections of short stories, six novels, another six volumes of poetry, several books of literary criticism, and at least one autobiographical volume.

99 The Tent (Al-Khiba') by Miral al-Tahawy (1996)

This was the author's acclaimed debut novel, and noted as the first to throw a light on Bedouin life from the perspective of a young woman. Miral al-Tahawy's Bedouin background is mirrored in the experience of her heroine Fatima and the telling of everyday stories about the lives and struggles of women in patriarchal society. To the young Fatima, five years old at the start of the story, the women collude in their own oppression, among them her harsh witch of a grandmother and her mother, traumatised by her inability to produce a live son. Fatima rebelled by being a tomboy and living between reality and fantasy, with her genie and her imagination.

Miral al-Tahawi, born in 1970 in the Sharqia Governorate of Egypt, is regarded as a pioneering woman novelist and short-story writer. Of Bedouin heritage, she has illuminated the issues and contradictions of living in modern-day society. With her progressive father ensuring that she was educated, she was able to gain a BA degree, work as a school teacher and then study at Cairo University for an MA and PhD, and acquiring Persian, Hebrew and English languages, before moving to the USA, where she is presently associate professor at Arizona State University. Her fourth novel, *Brooklyn Heights* (2010), won her the 2010 Naguib Mahfouz Medal for Literature and was shortlisted for the 2011 IPAF.

100 Al-Sudd (The Dam) by Mahmoud Messadi (1940)

Set within a vast and remote desert land in an unknown time and place, Messadi's celebrated work brings to life a series of contemporary existential concepts embedded in ancient Islamic mysticism, while evoking the suspense and philosophical dimensions of a Greek tragedy. Protagonist Ghaylan and his wife Maymouna find themselves in an infertile valley living with a community who worship the Goddess of Drought. Ghaylan seeks to build a

dam to give new life to the land and people, and save them from drought, famine, misery and epidemics. When accidents and mishaps happen to Ghaylan, his wife believes it is because he is challenging the gods. In a storm the dam fails but Ghaylan still stands, like Prometheus, Gilgamesh, Sisyphus or Greek gods. Praised as a masterpiece by Taha Hussein, particularly for its rconciliation between Islam and existentialism as Messadi reflects on complex questions of human will.

STEPHAN MILICH

The Poet as Excavator:
Ghassan Zaqtan's Museum of Words

In regions where wars, massacres and other violent events leave behind them devastated landscapes and lifeless bodies and souls, the function of poetry often converges with that of archaeology, which tries to uncover the past, and give findings that have a coherent and comprehensible meaning and narrative. This process of producing meaning becomes almost impossible to realize without contextual knowledge, without personal memory, and without historiography which mainly does justice to the victor. The task to "excavate" a place becomes utterly impossible when the poet excavator is not even allowed to visit or stay there, as in the case of the majority of Palestinians who were expelled from their land, which was subsequently confiscated by Israel. When there is no direct access to a place, when what remains there is not sufficient, and when neither memory nor history can provide an adequate frame for understanding, the poet can only imagine the lost world that constantly projects into the present, burdening life with a despotic legacy. The foundation for this imaginative creation, poiesis, is made from all the senses, turning the wandering poet into a recipient of aural and visual signals, signs and hints.

It is for this reason that the poetic world of Ghassan Zaqtan, the Palestinian poet and writer, is imbued with the absent, the buried and the unseen. Displaced from a land whose past had already been physically extinguished before the poet's birth in 1954, the memory

Ghassan Zaqtan

of the grown-ups, of elder family members — especially his mother — became the vital source for the creation of the young boy's world and imagination, no matter how fragmented, incomplete and ide-- alized were the memories of the others. In a certain proximity to Jacques Derrida's use of the word "trace" (*athar*), the remains turn into a track, a path or corridor through which the poet has to travel in order to discover, and then revive, the absent and the lost, bearing the doubtfulness that becomes his constant companion. Yet at the same time, in naming the absent, the lost or destroyed, its opposite is evoked: that once intact landscape or house in which a family had lived, a family whose expulsion, destruction and loss symbolize the unredeemed injustice continuing to haunt and shape a present that is still adrift.

Therefore, the points of departure for a great number of poems by Ghassan Zaqtan are deserted places, ruins and landscapes. Hills, canyons, trees, walls, attics and arches of ruined houses can be resurrected in the imagination of the poet, precisely because the poet returned to his "last exile", the West Bank, in 1994. There he wanders through a homeland defaced by "the bulldozers of history"[1] and reconstructed by the occupation. Instead of violent acts of naming, thereby appropriating both reality and land, it is listening, with all senses attuned, to obscure, barely perceptible sounds, shadows and voices, that becomes the highest virtue of the poet excavator. This is especially true in his poetry collection Istidraj al-jabal (Luring the Mountain), published in 1999, that is to a certain extent the outcome of that "return" from exile – but more importantly, to his family's village Zakariyya, situated within Israel today.[2] What appears first, after the poet's incomplete arrival or imaginative "return" to Palestine, is the apparition of sounds, gestures and animated objects, and of houses that seem to be haunted by ghosts. These undead indicate the necessity of "learning to live with the spectre" as Derrida programmatically claimed in his *Les Spectres de Marx* (1993). The poetic imagination, thus, has to depart from *places*, eager to write a "topical history" in which "places remember events", as James Joyce wrote in early drafts of *Ulysses*.[3] The events, however, cannot be recalled any more. No such story can be told from beginning to the end, nor can it be narrated in heroic mode.

The poems can only evoke fragments of memory, fading sounds – and only poetry can make landscapes and deserted houses speak, putting fragmented memories and remnants into an order that tries to do justice to the past. In refusing to create a grand narrative by choosing the fragment as the main poetic form, the poet aims at deconstructing both the Israeli and Palestinian grand narratives, thereby creating a new kind of silent nostalgia. In accordance with this poetic vision which rather listens than speaks out, the poetics of small details and precise description has replaced the loud symbolism of traditional resistance poetry.

In this sense, the title *Istidraj al-jabal* (1999) can be interpreted in three ways, all of them in the form of the genitive of the object: "climbing the mountain", "luring/seducing the mountain" and "bringing the mountain to do something", namely speaking to an exile who has only insufficient memories of Zakariyya – only a few blurred photographs remaining. Zaqtan explained this lack of re-maining memories and signs in an essay, published in April 1997 in Mahmoud Darwish's cultural journal *al-Karmel*: "Suddenly, I did not have anything I could rely on: no scenario, no house, no tree. What in Palestine was indeed available for me to document my past was too scarce, too obscure and to insufficient [...]."[4] The title could also be rendered in the genitive of the subject, "the call of the moun-tain", creating a complex dialectic between the landscape and the returnee.

A number of Zaqtan's poems can thus be read as poetic encoun-ters with "Erinnerungslandschaften", memoryscapes, that were not present, were not accessible at the distance of exile and could not be brought to mind in an act of creating the present – 'presentifi-cation' (*istihdar*). In the trilogy *'Auda* (Return), consisting of three poems, the trajectory of a family or a group of exiles – since the poem speaks in the first person plural – returning to the land is re-ported in a highly elliptic, fragmented and vague way:

Return I

The deep scars in the land
the fear in the stammering of the arches
the suitable carpet on the soil
the garden at night
the bridge down at the road's bend.
We have not arrived yet.

(*My translation*)

It is not enough to physically arrive at a place. In order to fully arrive, it needs more than just to a physical return to the homeland, which is now barely recognizable. All signs the viewer mentions in-dicate the non-arrival of the returning "we". The land is still wounded; the fear not further specified has been preserved in the architecture, and although the carpet seems to be appropriate for prayer, the speaker of the poem has to admit that "we have not ar-rived yet". The only action that is mentioned is the negation of ar-rival. The relation between the "we" and the place is still one of strangeness.

The second poem, *Return II*, leads us into the interior of an abandoned house still animated by the life of its former inhabitants:

Return II

They are no more here
but the fireplaces are still warm
the silk lies on the ground
. . . smell of sleep and straw obscures the place
there is a sound one can hear, like a plant clashing with a horse
what remained
or what has been effused by the sound of the tambourines
they are no more here
but the tables were put along the wall
all bottles empty
and the glasses
still at their place . . .
like murdered flowers slumbering in the shelf.

Those who lived there are no more there, but they left their un-
canny traces enabling the imaginative reconstruction of a moment
of flight: the fireplace still warm, silk fallen to the ground, some
sleeping on mattresses of straw, as well as tables, bottles and glasses
hinting at a daily routine that was supposedly interrupted by a sud-

den danger forcing the residents to depart hastily. Comparing the glasses to murdered flowers, the poem carefully alludes to the act of killing the beauty and vitality of the earlier daily village life, now conserved in the poem. In the absence of an internationally recognized museum[5] for the presentation of modern Palestinian history and, more specifically, for the silenced memories of the Nakba, which would document and display the lost rural and urban life of Palestinians in a non-heroic way, it is poetry that transforms the reader into a visitor, inviting him or her to wander through landscapes of perception: landscapes made up of remaining and imagined sounds, smells, views and tactile stimuli, all of which carefully evoke feelings and thoughts in order to change our attitude and perspective on the past, aiming to modify our relation to reality by trying to make us see, listen to and take seriously what and who are the absent and the suppressed.

If we are ready to see, if we want to see and put an end to continuous repression, the potential for a different life emerges only after the ghosts of the past have been buried, which allows them to rest in peace, or, at least, after one has "learn[ed] to live with ghosts, in the upkeep, the conversation, the company, the companionship, without commerce of ghosts". (Derrida 1994, xviii)

The third and final poem, Return III, illustrates that this burial has to take place inside the house – and not on a graveyard – in order to let the current inhabitants restore their peace of mind:

Return III

Something happens
The air high above trembles
at the silhouettes of the ruins
Silent flaps seem to touch each other
steps, maybe
a call

The ancestors have returned
in order to put themselves to rest in the attic.

While the first two poems are dominated by potentiality, the last poem is governed by certainty. There exists a semantic correspondence between "house" and "poetic verse" – both *bait* in Arabic – as the house is the poem, or in the words of Mahmoud Darwish, "as the land is the language".[6] In the absence of intact houses, landscapes and museums that didn't survive or didn't come into being, poetry becomes the last refuge for an entropic past that still rules despotically over the present and future. This state of entropy has to be put into order again, by "ontologizing the remains" (Derrida 1994) and by making the landscapes speak.

The poetry of Ghassan Zaqtan is searching for ghosts and the dead who turn into a medium to restore truth and justice. It is an attempt to claim the past without falling into the trap of constructing a new myth or narrative. For the same reason, Zaqtan's poetry does not accuse or fight the Other, the "enemy", but tries to hint at the pains caused by expulsion, negation and the various forms of ongoing violence.

Ghassan Zaqtan's collection *Istidraj al-jabal* (Luring the Mountain) is published by Al-Muassasaa al-arabiya lil-Dirassat wal-Nashr, Amman, Beirut, 1999.

NOTES:

1 This expression by Mahmoud Darwish alludes to the task of the poet who has to "guard language from being emptied of the voices of the victims who ask for their share in tomorrow's memory". See Darwish: In the Presence of Absence (tr. Sinan Antoon). New York: Archipelago 2011, 126.'

2 The village Zakariyya in the Hebron District counted 1180 inhabitants in 1944/45. The village was finally taken on 23 October 1948, but "unlike most of the inhabitants of villages conquered in these operations, the villagers were not displaced at the time of the operation". (Khalidi 1992, 226) The process of depopulation lasted until 1950, although – according to a note by an Israeli ministry official – the village comprised "'many good houses, and it is possible to accommodate in them several hundred new immigrants'" (Walidi 1992, 226). In 1950, the settlement of Zekharya was established. The state of the old village at the end of the 1980s is described as follows: "The mosque and a number of houses, some occupied by Jewish residents and other deserted, remain on the site. Large sections of the site itself are covered with wild vegetation. [...] One of the occupied houses is a two-storey stone structure with a flat roof. Its second storey windows have round arches [...]." (Walidi 1992, 226)

3 See Paul Ricoeur: La Memoire, l'Histoire, l'Oubli. Paris: Editions du Seuil 2000, 188.

4 Zaqtan, Nafi l-manfa (The Negation of Exile) in: al-Karmel 51, (Ramallah) April 1997, 141-145.

5 Although the "Palestinian Museum" opened in 2016 at Birzeit, the original plan "to create a museum dedicated to the memory of the Nakba in order to document the catastrophe" was finally abandoned. The museum is now dedicated "to celebrate Palestine's culture more broadly", with a first exhibition on Jerusalem by various artists. See the Museum's website: http://www.palmuseum.org/about/the-museum.

6 This is also the title of the famous documentary film on Mahmoud Darwish by Simone Bitton, taken from a line of Darwish's poetry.

BASSAM FRANGIEH

Hanna Mina: Pioneer of Social Realism in Modern Arabic Literature

Hanna Mina was one of the foremost novelists of the Arab world, renowned for his depiction of the social tensions and hard realities of life in modern Syria, as well as the lives of sailors and the sea. He excelled in depicting the afflictions of a life lived under great stress and anxiety, himself one of only a few major Arab writers to have suffered extreme poverty and hardship in his childhood and youth.

A leading Arab novelist, a pioneer in modern Arabic literature, and a leading force in the creation and development of the Arabic novel, Hanna Mina was born in 1924 in Lattakia, Syria. He died in Damascus, Syria on August 21, 2018, at the age of 94. The eminent Syrian writer had narrated not only his life, as well as the life of the poor, the marginalized, and the oppressed; but also recorded the social and political developments and the cultural history of Syria following the First World War. As a particularly productive and genuine realist, he became the front-runner of the social realism trend in modern Arab prose.

Mina was a self-taught writer and a self-made man. He attended only a few years of elementary school before he was forced to drop out and look for work, in order to provide for his family. As a boy he worked, amongst other jobs, in a barber shop: he swept the floor, dumped the trash, and prepared tea for customers. He suffered hunger, displacement, and homelessness. He lived on the streets for years, leading him to become a friend to and advocate of the homeless, the oppressed, the deprived and the banished.

He worked as a porter and janitor in seaports; later he became a sailor, establishing a profound relationship with the sea. The sweat of the suffering sailors and deprived workers, the cooling breeze of the sea, the refreshing and uplifting waves and blue depths of the sea – all these impressions and experiences fed into his work, leading him to be called "the novelist of the sea", because of its central place in his writing.

In 1942, Mina began writing short stories for literary magazines in Syria and Lebanon, and in 1947 he decided to leave the barber shop in Lattakia and move to Damascus to begin his career in journalism. He played a major role in establishing the Syrian Writers Union in 1951; he also helped shape its ideology, emphasizing the social and political commitment of the Arab writer — an idea that was very influential in Arabic literature in the post-independence climate of the 1950s. He contributed to the foundation of the Arab Writers Union in 1969.

Mina's first novel *Blue Lamps* opened a new phase in his career; after its publication in 1954 he devoted himself exclusively to writing novels. The novel remained his principle obsession and favorite literary form of writing; yet he continued to publish short stories and other literary and journalistic essays and articles. Mina continued to express in his writings the voice of resistance against the European powers, particularly the French colonizers; believing that the novel must reflect social reality, as it is the most suitable genre for the articulation and transformation of personal and social reality.

He produced 40 works, mostly novels; several of his novels were made into admired films, and turned into popular television series. In appreciation of his role as a leading Syrian writer, Mina was offered a position in the Syrian Ministry of Culture. In 1966 he published *The Sail and the Storm*, in which he exposed the exploitation of seaport workers by the French colonizers and their French local agents, and called for resistance and defiance. *Fragments of Memory* (1974) and *The Swamp* (1977), two autobiographical novels narrated from a child's point of view, narrate the experiences of his own sadly deprived childhood.

After the publication of his third novel, *Snow Comes through the Window* (1969), which emphasized the need for political activism, defiance and revolt in life, Mina received the Award of The Syrian State. His literary achievements brought him several other presti-

HANNA MINA

SUN ON A CLOUDY DAY

Translated by
Bassam Frangieh and Clementina Brown

An Original From Passeggiata Press

gious awards, among them the Sultan Owais Cultural Foundation award in Abu Dhabi in 1990, the Arab Writer's Prize for his collected works in 2005, and the Mohamed Zafzaf Prize for Arabic Literature in 2010.

Mina's novel *Sun on a Cloudy Day* (1973) is considered by critics to be one of the most important novels in Arabic literature. It accurately portrays the social and political conflict, class struggle and contradictions which prevailed in Syria during the French Mandate. Mina communicated his vision beyond the borders of Syria and its mandate, to apply to every society under an oppressive regime; in this way, the novel is universal. The dagger-dancer in the novel is seeking to reach the truth, and to achieve the justice that is as inevitable as the sun rising, despite the thick black clouds blocking its rays. An observer described the dagger-dance in the novel as a symbolic challenge and confrontation, a fierce fight with life and its violence, and a strong affirmation of human existence.

In this novel, as well as in his other novels, Mina tells us that we must beat the earth until she wakes up. We must learn how to lose ourselves in something which generates and creates real passion. Mina wrote, "Life is beautiful. Drink from its spring; what seems muddy today will become clear as crystal tomorrow." In his novels, Mina brought to our consciousness a simple but important truth: we must have someone or something to live for, because living for nothing is false. "Only then do playing, singing, and dancing have meaning." Mina believes that if we do not possess something we are devoted to, then we must create it, even only in our imagination. According to Mina, sincerity and devotion are the ultimate keys to joy. To devote oneself to something means to love it. As a result, when we give our heart and soul to something, it will give itself to us. He wrote, "Let your instruments speak if you are a musician. Let your feet speak if you are a dancer. Let your arms speak if you are a fighter." He insisted that the key to success lies in persevering with devotion. "Persevering is the key," and that we must "keep beating our sleeping land with our feet to wake her up, and she shall be awoken. The door that is knocked on shall open. And the magic spell dissolve when we act sincerely." Mina's works are like paintings, revealing themselves fully only upon contemplation.

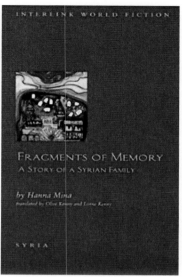

Mina is never a silent witness. Ever truthful to his values and philosophies in life and art, he endured imprisonment and exile due to his principles and views. He stood in the gutter with the deceived and the powerless. His protagonists refuse to reconcile with their depressed reality. They are always revolting against miserable, unjust conditions. Mina, a genuine social realist with social and moral commitment, used his pen as a weapon to create new consciousness; which is a first step toward any revolutionary change, and a necessary requirement for eradicating misery and oppression. As a writer, he sought to change the existing order of a society that was besieged by inhumane conditions, striving above all for cultural, political, and social change in Arab life. He became a literary school unto himself, a school of genuine realism mixed with revolutionary idealism, unique in the history of Arabic literature.

Mina was a legend in life and literature. He raged against colonialism, corruption and injustice across the Middle East. He was the first Arabic writer to use genuine social realism in modern Arabic prose writing. He was a writer with a passionate concern for changing the existing order of Arab society. His legacy and literature have significantly influenced the modern Arab novel. His departure leaves a chasm in modern Arabic prose literature — an emptiness likely to continue for a long time. There seem to be no contemporary writers following in his footsteps, let alone any who could fill the void his passing has left.

Susannah Tarbush *reviews*

**Sophia: or,
The Beginning of All Tales
by Rafik Schami**
Translated from the German by
Monique Arav and John Hannon
Interlink Books, Northampton, USA, 2018
ISBN: 9781566560313. Pbk, 480pp, $20.00 / £14.95

Framed by the very structure of the clan

In this exuberant novel, the Syrian-German author Rafik Schami weaves an intricate tapestry of love, sectarianism, exile, oppression and revolution, extending from the late 1920s to early 2011. The rich 444-page non-linear narrative presents a multitude of characters and storylines in settings from Damascus, Homs and Beirut to Rome and the German city of Heidelberg

Schami was born in Damascus in 1946 and migrated to Germany in 1971 for political reasons. He has built a reputation as a master storyteller, with the publication since the early 1980s of a stream of novels, short stories, children's books, plays and essays. He has won numerous awards, and his work has been translated from German into many languages.

Sophia: or, The Beginning of All Tales is the most recent of three big multigenerational family sagas Schami has produced this century: *Die dunkle Seite der Liebe* (2004) *Das Geheimnis des Kalligraphen* (2008) and *Sophia oder Der Anfang aller Geschichten* (2015). All are published by Hanser Verlag of Munich.

The first two titles were translated into English by Anthea Bell. They were published in the US by Interlink Books, and in the UK by Arabia Books, as *The Dark Side of Love* (2009, excerpted in *Banipal 31*) and *The Calligrapher's Secret* (2011, excerpted in *Banipal 39* and reviewed by André Naffis-Sahely in *Banipal 40*).

The English translation of *Sophia* by Monique Arav and John Hannon reads well, although there are occasional infelicities, for example in word choice or order.

At the core of the novel are three main characters: Karim, Sophia, and Sophia's son Salman. Karim, a Muslim, was born in Homs in 1927. As a youth he fell madly in love with Sophia, a bold and beautiful Christian. She returned his passion, though being careful to retain her virginity and making it clear that she intended to marry a wealthy Christian. She duly married a rich Damascene goldsmith.

After Karim moves to Damascus as a schoolteacher in 1950, he and Sophia conduct a secret affair. His life is plunged into turmoil when he is framed by his own family for the honour killing of his sister and the Christian husband with whom she had eloped. Sophia saves Karim by taking him to the home of her aged aunt, who harbours him until he is no longer hunted by the authorities. Karim is deeply grateful to Sophia for all her efforts on his behalf and tells her: "How can I ever repay you? I would do anything for you, even die." But to Sophia's dismay Karim insists on ending their affair when he gets married and promises his wife that he will be a faithful husband.

The search for freedom, whether personal, social or political, is a recurring theme of *Sophia*. Karim is a liberated free thinker. In the opening scene of *Sophia*, set in Damascus in summer 2006, he is teaching his lover Aida to ride a bicycle down Jasmine Street, in the Christian quarter. It is six months since the couple first met and fell in love. Karim is in his early eighties, Aida in her mid-fifties, and both have been widowed for many years.

The late-blooming love between Karim and Aida and their public displays of affection bring much criticism in the neighbourhood, partly because he is a Muslim, she a Christian. Karim counters hostile questions with "I'm not a Muslim, a Christian, a Druze, or a Jew. Love is my religion, do you understand?"

Karim and Aida first met at a monthly meeting of "the Selfless", described as "peaceful idealists who meet to sing, eat and hold discussions". They are followers of al-Hakim, author of a subversive book entitled The Fortress of Love. "Every line, every word, was a call to resist dictatorship and its loss of freedom and dignity." Al-Hakim was said to have been murdered.

In the novel's second chapter the focus switches to Sophia's son Salman, who is the wealthy owner of a food import-export business living in exile in Rome with his Italian wife Stella and 15-year-old son Paulo. Salman had realised long before, during his first marriage to a German woman, that he is unable to form a mature relationship with one woman. His erotic life in Rome combines his cooled marriage with a series of infatuations and sexual adventures.

As a young graduate in Syria, in 1967 Salman had joined an underground armed anti-government group. He fled the country in 1970 on counterfeit travel documents, having shot and wounded a policeman in an attack on a police station. He is still worried that the policeman may have died of his injuries.

His escape took him first to Beirut to stay with his paternal aunt Amalia. She had been shunned by her brothers 30 years earlier for marrying the Lebanese Protestant academic she loved, rather than a Syrian Catholic. She tells Salman that as long as young revolutionaries like him fight only for social or political change, their struggle will be futile. "No change will ever come to Arab countries until the very structure of the clan that enslaves us, body and soul, has been destroyed." Salman grew painfully disillusioned with his former revolutionary activities.

In summer 2010 Salman becomes obsessed by the idea of returning to Damascus after his long years of absence, being increasingly distracted by his memories of that city. But he distrusts an amnesty for past political offences that the Syrian government had issued earlier that year. His aged parents approach his cousin Elias, who had been a guerrilla with Salman but is now a senior officer in the Syrian secret service. Elias keeps them dangling for months until, after Salman's father pays him $10,000, he assures the family that there are no records against Salman in the 15 departments of the secret service, or at border posts.

Salman flies to Damascus in December 2010 and is brought up against the realities of the Assad regime. Schami casts a satirical eye

Rafik Schami, photo by Root Leeb

over the upper echelons of Damascene society as he describes Salman's realisation that many of his revolutionary comrades from the 1960s are now colluding with the regime and prospering.

But Salman is forced to go on the run after *Tishrin* newspaper publishes his photo with a report that he is wanted for the murder of Fatima Haddad, wife of the culture minister and former head of the secret service. Salman suspects that Elias is somehow involved in publication of this fake news. After all, even during their days as armed militants, some of the revolutionaries had suspected Elias of being a traitor.

Like Karim, six decades earlier, he is on the run, framed for a murder he did not commit, and desperately in need of a safe hiding place. Sophia visits the now elderly Karim to beg for his help, and Karim agrees to give Salman refuge. He tries to come up with a plan to enable Salman to escape the country. Salman has been told by his cousin Tarek that Sophia had once saved Karim's life, and that Karim had promised to return the favour. When Salman asks Karim why he is risking his life for him, Karim recalls his old love story with Sophia, whom he describes as "the beginning of all tales".

At one point Salman visits former comrade-in-arms Hani, who has suffered years of imprisonment. In the most harrowing chapter of *Sophia* Hani tells Salman of the incarceration and torture he endured, particularly at the hands of Elias: ". . . An entire city of hell lies beneath Damascus, seven floors down, and spreads out . . . It's hundreds of kilometres wide and it mushrooms out of the ground in Adra, Saidnaya, and Palmyra. There are camps and prisons there for hundreds and thousands of innocent people. This hell is so well organized that the people who live above ground can't hear or feel it."

Sophia ends in early 2011, just as the "Arab Spring" is beginning. It is a novel that makes it amply clear why Syria was at that time a tinder box, waiting for a spark to ignite it.

Becki Maddock reviews

Tales of Yusuf Tadrus
by Adel Esmat
Translated by Mandy McClure

Published by Hoopoe Fiction, Cairo, 30 March 2018 - ISBN 78-9774168604. Pbk, 216pp, £9.99 / USD $19.99, Kindle £7.19 / USD $9.37

Yusuf Tadrus says: "Art is a source of both grief and joy"

E smat's novel takes the form of Yusuf Tadrus, the introspective and troubled protagonist, telling the tale of his life to an unidentified interlocutor, in chapters, which each begin: "Yusuf Tadrus says".

The novel is refreshing in two ways, its setting and the protagonist. Unlike the majority of Egyptian novels, *Tales of Yusuf Tadrus* is not set in Cairo or Alexandria, rather the majority of Yusuf's tale takes place in the provincial cities of Tanta, in the Nile Delta, and El-Tur, in Sinai. Furthermore, the protagonist is a Christian. Through him Esmat charts Egypt's socio-economic and religious evolution since the 1960s. Yusuf's own personal story tells much of what life has been like for ordinary Egyptians since this time, but Yusuf also occasionally makes comments on the significant political and economic events, remarking for example: "That was in the summer of 1977, the beginning of the inflation that nipped away at people's wages, the beginning of the collapse of services." There is an element of nostalgia in these comments: "That was in the mid-1960s – the city wasn't like it is now."

Through Yusuf, Esmat addresses issues of religion and sheds light on the experience of being a Christian in modern Egypt, which, as

Adel Esmat

elsewhere in the Middle East, experiences religious tensions. Yusuf observes a dangerous trend of Muslims living among Muslims and Christians among Christians, remarking: "By that time, in the mid-1990s, most of the girls were veiled and the sorting had begun . . . the general mood started tilting towards segregation."

Yusuf himself suffers from persecution at work because of his faith. In the "grim atmosphere of the 1990s", after a forbidden love affair with a Muslim colleague, he is banished to a job in El-Tur, where, "[i]n that remote spot, my Christianity stalked me as well". His son Michel also suffers. "His tale was a retelling of the story of persecution generation after generation", causing Michel to be focused on "getting away from here".

Alongside the specifically Egyptian experiences, Yusuf experiences more universal dilemmas. His religion is just one aspect of the identity crisis he suffers: "I'm not the person whose face they see . . . Who am I? . . . humanity's problem since the dawn of consciousness." Yusuf is looking for peace of mind, his place in the world, himself. Fascinated from a young age by light and shadow, he finds in painting a way of resisting society's rigidity and conformity and his obsession with his face and the search for the self leads Yusuf to paint ninety-nine self-portraits as he searches for himself in his face.

However, there is a conflict between his desire to paint and his own and others' expectations, the pressure to provide for his family, to put away childish things, to conform, do what is expected, embrace the conventional life and like many of us he realises later than by doing so he has lost something of himself. Yusuf's lack of means leads him to give up studying Fine Arts at the University of Alexandria and return home to Tanta, where he marries and works as a teacher and struggles to provide for his family. Esmat vividly depicts the way life and the expectations of others and oneself take over

from youthful passions, which remain under the surface, making one feel one is not being true to oneself or truly oneself.

Yusuf also talks about fear, which he describes as "an illness I still haven't recovered from." Aged seven, Yusuf was struck by a lorry and "the accident blew out some coping centre, a kind of fear settled inside me". Painting helps him to deal with this anxiety. His art teacher tells him "Paint what you wish. Don't be afraid" and he says "[m]aybe I've associated painting with a lack of fear ever since.", while noting that "[p]ainting does not rid a person of fear, but it makes fear trivial, tolerable." He wishes he "could paint the terror of the day of the accident to rid myself of it, but that's contrived."

Mandy McClure has produced a very readable translation of a novel that combines history, human experience and philosophical musings. McClure is the translator of *Arab Women Writers: A Critical Reference Guide* (AUC Press, 2008) and co-translator of *The Traditional Crafts of Egypt* (AUC Press, 2016). She lives in Cairo.

Adel Esmat was born in the Gharbiya Governorate of Egypt in 1959. He graduated in philosophy from the Faculty of Arts of Cairo's Ain Shams University in 1984. He lives in Tanta and works as a library specialist in the Egyptian Ministry of Education. *Tales of Yusuf Tadrus* won the 2016 Naguib Mahfouz Medal for Literature. It is Esmat's fifth novel.

Yusuf's "Tales" are not just of himself but also of Egypt and Egyptians, about which the author does not present a positive picture. For example, when Yusuf returns to Tanta he remarks, "by then the city was teeming with humanity. You couldn't find a place to put your foot." "Can you believe we used to complain of what the infitah, liberalization, had done in the 1980s? We didn't know worse was coming." Yusuf's final plea at the end of the novel is: "Tell me, for God's sake, when will the light shine on this country?"

Ruth Padel reviews

A Boat to Lesbos and Other Poems by Nouri Al-Jarrah

translated by Camilo Gómez-Rivas
and Allison Blecker,
with paintings by Reem Yassouf.

Banipal Books, London, 2018
ISBN 7890995636941. Pbk, 120pp, £9.99 / USD16.97

The cry of the grieving survivor

The island of Lesbos, also called Mytilene, is on the edge of Europe. You see Turkey three and a half miles away, on the hazy horizon. Being so close to Troy, it suffered in the Trojan war: Achilles plundered its cities, and nine of its beautiful women were offered to him in an attempt to end his quarrel with Agamemnon. Until 2015, though, the island was most famous for three things; its petrified forest, the best ouzo in Greece, and poetry. The head of Orpheus supposedly washed up there, and in the seventh century BC two geniuses, Alcaeus and his younger contemporary Sappho, inaugurated the Western lyric tradition. Both belonged to the governing aristocracy and both spent time in exile: Sappho, supposedly, in Sicily.

Since September 2015, Lesbos has become world famous as a tragic frontline for refugees. Over a million Syrians arrived in small rubber dinghies, escaping war in Syria. Their journeys and deaths, the people smugglers exploiting them, their orange life jackets (sold extortionately in Turkey but often not even sea-worthy) littering the island's shores, made headlines over the world.

Now a Syrian poet has forged his own unforgettable lyrics from those landings and from the myths, history, poetry and tragedy already surrounding the island. The delicate, heart-breaking poems in *A Boat to Lesbos* find in Sappho's exile a common bond between the island's most famous poet and Syrians escaping civil war. You fight for life on the boats, says Sappho's voice, and the sea swallows you before you land in Lesbos, while I die in Sicily fleeing home. Out of the love lyrics which Sappho made famous, there are still further links possible to dream: 'Sappho, lover of youth, here are your young/ lovers from Syria. They come to you silently, / lightly, / And their beauty is a flash of lightning that dwells in a window. / Set the table for them/ and confess that this is their last supper.'

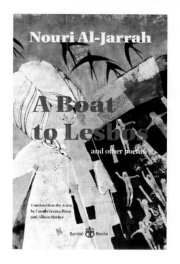

Nouri Al-Jarrah is an important Arab voice in Europe. He was born in Damascus in 1956 and has lived in London since he was thirty. These poems, published in Arabic by the Milan-based al-Mutawassit Press in 2016, are in many voices but underneath all of them is the cry of the grieving survivor. In 'A Boat in the Harbour', for instance, dated 'Lesbos, 2nd August 2016,' we read, 'That's me, there, / as if a ghost, or spectre, or vision/ a trace/ of/ the cry/ of someone drowning, / and my reflection in the bathroom mirror/ of the hotel/ at the port/ is only the face of one who sailed and did not return.' Sometimes we hear the voice of a Greek tablet, Greek traveller or writers, but all the poems move towards a final cry of guilt and loss, that the poet was not there to share his city's pain.

'I wasn't in Damascus when the earthquake hit, / I wasn't on a mountain or a plain, / when the earth shook, images cracked, / and the world split apart.'

These poems weave exile, death and the sea into many journey myths. Not only Greek journeys, but the Daughters of Na'sh, an alternative Arabic name for al-Dubb al-Akbar, Big Bear, the seven stars which the West calls the Big Dipper or Ursa Major.

In myth, Na'sh was killed by Canopus, who fled to the southern hemisphere. His daughters will not bury him until they have been revenged on his killer, so there the stars are, seven daughters, forever carrying their father's coffin. A haunting image for the survivors of September 2015. 'Suffering Syrians, beautiful Syrians,

Nouri al-Jarrah

Syrian brothers/ fleeing death. You won't reach the shores on rafts/ but will be born on beaches with the foam.'

The book throbs also with nostalgia for Damascus. 'I'll sit with you in the garden and you'll sit with me in my dream . . ./ I'll write to you, Damascus, imprisoned behind the sun. Damascus is far more present, here, than the hills of Lesbos. I stand in the Umayyad court-yard/ and flagellate myself with chains, says one poem. I am in this small port/ here in Lesbos,/ in thrall to the smell of the sea,/ my hair all over my face/ and my hands, pierced by light,/ asking tourists and refugees/ about my fugitive face/ and gouged eyes.'

In September 2016, I revisited Lesbos myself, I must have arrived just as Al-Jarrah left, for his poems with a Lesbos by-line are dated August 2016. Greece was in recession, many islanders could not even afford coffee but evening restaurants were full of foreign aid workers, who could afford food which Lesbos islanders cannot. Everywhere I saw potential ingredients for resentment against refugees. And yet cafés offered free charging for mobile phones, and graffiti said "Refugees welcome". This was due not only to Greek hospitality and humanity, but to memories of the Smyrna Catastro-phe, 1922, when Greeks fled massacre in burning Izmir and came mostly to Lesbos, where they became grandparents of the current generation. I talked to a newspaper editor who had waited for dinghies in the dark and pulled Syrian children from the waves, and said their stories were exactly like those told by her grandmother, who escaped from Smyrna as a child.

Nouri Al-Jarrah brackets the destruction of Izmir with the fall of Troy: 'Thanks to this sea/ to sad Izmir/ to the virgin wave/ that bore me from my mother's arms/ to give me back the earth/ rot the earth, for all earth, from this day, to be my grave./ Thanks to my gods who died on the ramparts/ to Troy that burned/ to the Greek ships that didn't see me.'

His Lesbos is the place where death and wreckage wash up, like the head of Orpheus. 'I wasn't in Damascus/ I wasn't in Damas-cus./ And now/ at the end of the Earth/ I listen to a waterwheel weeping in the orchard/ and the wind describing it to the moun-tain.'

A Boat to Lesbos is a voyage to the place where loss is forever made manifest.

Peter Kalu reviews
Baghdad Noir
edited by Samuel Shimon

Akashic Noir Series, Akashic Books, USA,
September 2018
ISBN 978-1617753435. Pbk, 256pp. £11.99 /
USD10.97.   Kindle £11.39/ USD 14.90

A multidimensional, many-voiced, defiant collection

This new Akashic Noir, *Baghdad Noir*, contains fourteen new short stories penned by an impressive line-up of primarily Iraqi writers. Each story is set in a different part of Baghdad. The tales are a heterogenous bunch: in 'I Killed Her Because I Loved Her', a mother and her two daughters are working on different sides of the American forces v Insurgency divide, with tragic consequences. In 'Doomsday Book', a man is recruited to commit "divine, holy murder" until his distraught brother tracks down the recruiter. In 'Baghdad on Borrowed Time', a detective is hired by a killer with a bizarre proposition: the killer wants himself killed. In 'The Apartment', a sharp-eyed criminal investigator detects an old lady's death was not by natural causes. In 'Empty Bottles', a young woman is murdered, her screams masked by the call to morning prayers, as an entire neighbourhood blocks its ears. In 'Homecoming' a father is attacked by an area thug, leaving his soldier son seething. In 'Baghdad House', an accountant lands up in a hotel with deadly goings-on. The overall effect of this gathering of stories is kaleidoscopic: shifting fragments that, coming together in the collection, create a sense of Baghdad's uneasily beating heart.

The stories are crisply edited. Most of the stories have been translated from Arabic, in smoothly accomplished translations, with three written in English.

Salima Saleh   Ahmed Saadawi   Hadia Said

As a city, Baghdad presents a challenge for crime fiction. Arguably, the genre is predicated on a functioning state apparatus imposing law (however cankered), and handing down some form of justice, (however partial or temporary), against a backdrop of a society in some form of order (however warped). Given all these anchors — law, justice, order — appear to have been pulled apart by the maelstroms Iraq has experienced, the genre has to react. The *Baghdad Noir* response is to explore what justice might mean to citizens living in such a shattered landscape, how individuals either reconcile themselves to these disjunctions or else attempt to reconstitute justice and its associated concepts.

The collection features a wide range of such troubled, burdened protagonists: nervous accountants, embittered relatives, laconic detectives, traumatised children and frightened students among them. There are touches of the phantasmagorical and the magical in the tales but, for the most part, the mode is realist, as if the absurdities of life in Baghdad need no extra gilding with fantasy.

The moral tones found in the collection include existential, impersonal, ironic satirical, macabre, fatalistic, even a warped ecstatic; and the narrators swing from extra-diegetic, disengaged story-

Hussain al-Mozany 1954–2016

EDITED BY **SAMUEL SHIMON**

MUHSIN AL-RAMLI ✦ AHMED SAADAWI ✦ ALI BADER
SALIMA SALIH ✦ NASSIF FALAK ✦ SINAN ANTOON ✦ AND OTHERS

The fourteen stories are told by Sinan Antoon,
Ali Bader, Mohammed Alwan Jabr, Nassif Falak,
Dheya al-Khalidi, Hussain al-Mozany, Layla Qasrany,
Hayet Raies, Muhsin al-Ramli, Ahmed Saadawi,
Hadia Said, Salima Saleh, Salah Abdoh,
and Roy Scranton

www.akashicbooks.com

Layla Qasrany   *Mohammed Alwan Jabr*   *Sinan Antoon*

tellers to in-the-thick-of-it hero-protagonists. It is a superbly mul-
tidimensional, many-voiced, defiant collection.

The combination of short story mode and noir tone is particularly
effective. The short story as a form is at its best perhaps, when deal-
ing with unease and insecurity; it has an affinity with instability —
of self, family, region or nation. When to that is added the noir tone,
which shades the stories with a minor key of blue, the result is a
powerful set of stories that establish dialogue, speak the unspeak-
able, talk the pain, the fragments, the shared moments; they are a
movement towards reimagining and rebuilding this fractured city,
each story is a suture in the process.

In some sense, perhaps remarkably, this collection takes the short
story genre back to its roots. For example, the eighth story in *Bagh-*

dad Noir, Mohammed
Alwan Jabr's 'Room 22'
has many features in
common with Edgar
Allan Poe's seminal short
story, 'The Man of the
Crowd', perhaps the pre-
cursor of all crime fiction
and the story which led,
via Baudelaire, to the
term 'modernity' being
coined. Modern Baghdad
is served well by these
stories.

Ali Bader

Bill Swainson reviews
States of Passion
by Nihad Sirees
Translated by Max Weiss
Pushkin Press, London, 2018
ISBN: 9781782273479. Pbk, 256pp,
£12.99 / USD15.68

It was on a dark and stormy night . . .

Nihad Sirees is best known in the West as the author of the 2004 novel, *The Silence and the Roar*, translated into English by Max Weiss and published in the US by the Other Press and in the UK by Pushkin Press in 2013. An Orwellian parable with Kafkaesque overtones, it is set in an unnamed country in which the writer-narrator Fathi must choose between joining the loud chorus of approval for the country's leader and silence. Banned in Syria, *The Silence and the Roar* has also been translated into a number of other languages including Czech, Dutch, French, German Italian and Turkish.

Elsewhere in the world, especially in the Middle East, Sirees is better known as the creator of popular and challenging TV dramas, including *The Silk Market* (series 1, 23 parts, 1996; series 2, 25 parts, 1998), which explored Syria's union with Egypt in the late 1950s and early '60s through a wide range of characters in the Aleppo silk market. Also broadcast in Germany and Australia (with subtitles), the series was considered controversial by the Syrian government, and afterwards the threat of censorship meant that other TV dramas, including a life of Kahlil Gibran (2008) and *Al Khait Al Abiadh* (The First Gleam of Dawn, 2004), an unvarnished depiction of Syria's government-controlled media, had to be made outside the country. Following increasing surveillance and pressure from the government, Nihad Sirees left Syria in 2012, and after brief spells in Egypt and the USA now lives in Berlin.

It's worth rehearsing this literary biography, because Sirees' work for TV and several of his novels are concerned with history and politics, and it would be easy to characterise him as a writer of realist historical fiction – four of his seven novels, including his most recent, the novel of *The Silk Market* TV series (2005) fall into this category. However, his first novel, *The Cancer* (1987) and *The Silence and the Roar* (2004) do not. *States of Passion*, which has a contemporary setting but tells a

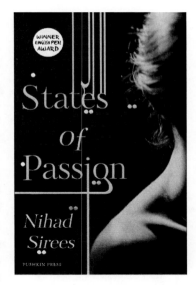

complicated love story from the 1930s, falls somewhere in between.

An unnamed bureaucrat working for the Agricultural Bank is on a field trip to a number of tiny villages with two colleagues when their Land Rover breaks down on a desert road in the middle of nowhere. As our expert was the one who proposed moving on to the next village that evening for an early start the following morning in hopes of a swift return to Aleppo, his two colleagues, who had been looking forward to warm hospitality where they were, are not best pleased. It's up to him to go and find help. Setting out in pouring rain, he soon finds himself surrounded by prowling dogs and, fearing for his life, is mightily relieved to find that an even larger pair of eyes up ahead turns out to be the lights of a substantial house. Inside an old man sits by the fire, while the butler opens the door. Once inside, the narrator remembers his stranded colleagues and while the butler reluctantly goes to look for them, the narrator, curiosity piqued, says in Max Weiss's English, which is most comfortable with narration, but veers rather unsteadily when attempting highly formal or colloquial speech:

"Tell me, respected sir, what made you come and live here? It may be impolite to ask but the question keeps nagging at me."

He raised his head, gazed at me with a gentle and resigned expression, and said:

"You have every right to ask, my new friend, but mine is a long

Nihad Sirees

story. It would take a very long time to hear the whole thing. To tell you the truth, I enjoy telling it, and would love to have someone around who wanted to hear my stories, but my butler keeps me from talking too much, because he says it's better for my health not to."

"Please, old man, tell me the story. Ever since I was a little boy, I've loved stories. I've craved hearing them."

And then the old man "began to tell his tale, which was strangest thing I had ever heard in my entire life".

The tale he tells on that dark and stormy night is the story of a doubly forbidden love affair between the old man in his youth and an innocent young dancer called Widad. Widad belongs to banat al-ishreh, the world of women who live, love, dance and play music together, which flourished in Aleppo of the 1930s, where, as the old man says, "women are with other women the same way that men are with women". This lesbian world that co-exists with the public world of marriage and children is affectionately evoked, and here Sirees's skill as a historical novelist comes to the fore, but it also has something of the feel of a film like Grand Hotel Budapest, which fun though it was, perhaps revelled to excess in its excesses.

Meanwhile, as the old man's story takes five days and nights to tell, the butler becomes increasingly determined to force the narrator to leave, fearful, among other things that it would be unfair to reveal here, that the old man will not survive the telling of the tale, but suffice to say that a scorpion, poison and a gun are involved.

If *The Silence and the Roar* is a modernist parable, then *States of Passion* has something of the feel of one of Sandor Marai's tales like *Embers* (1942, English translation by Carol Brown Janeway, 2001), or perhaps also the Turkish writer Sabahattin Ali's novel *Madonna in a Fur Coat* (1943, English translation by Maureen Freely with Alexander Dawe, 2017). But both of these novels succeed because in the first case the writer keeps to one story and a single, but engaging tone, and in the other because the love affair, with a similar time sequence to *States of Passion*, is utterly convincing. *States of Passion* presents an uneasy mix of narrative sophistication that doesn't quite come off and a love affair set in a historical world evoked as fantasy. Yet, something is happening here that makes me want to read what Nihad Sirees writes next from what he calls the 'disorder' of exile.

Chip Rossetti reviews

A Cloudy Day on the Western Shore
by Mohamed Mansi Qandil

Translated by Barbara Romaine

Syracuse University Press, October 2018
ISBN: 9780815611097. Pbk, 320pp, USD34.95/£26.64
ISBN: 9780815654629 Ebook, USD33.56 / £25.73.
http://syracuseuniversitypress.syr.edu/fall-2018/cloudy-day.html

Aisha meets Howard Carter

In a recent interview published in *Al-Ahram* newspaper, the Egyptian novelist Mohamed Mansi Qandil explained that in his writings he has followed the advice Naguib Mahfouz once gave him to "expand the working space of the Arabic novel so that it encompasses other regions". And indeed, the geographical settings of Qandil's novels range from Uzbekistan (*Moon over Samarqand*, 2004) to Mexico and Paris (*The Black Brigade*, 2016). His 2009 novel, *Yawm gha'im fi l-barr al-gharbi* (*A Cloudy Day on the Western Shore*), however, is set exclusively in Egypt, but plants itself in its past, alternating between the first decades of the 20th century and the reigns of Akhenaten and Tutankhamun. Shortlisted for the 2010 International Prize for Arabic Fiction (IPAF), the novel has now been published by Syracuse University Press in a beautiful English translation by Barbara Romaine.

Qandil manages to craft an appealing character in the protagonist, a young Egyptian peasant woman, Aisha, whose life intersects with a variety of well-known historical individuals, including political figures and noted Egyptologists. The novel opens on a desolate stretch of the Nile in Upper Egypt, where Aisha's mother hires a ferryman to take her and Aisha, then an adolescent, across the Nile. As the reader learns, her mother has stolen her away from their vil-

Mohamed Mansi Qandil

A Cloudy Day
on the Western Shore

Translated from the Arabic by Barbara Romaine

lage in order to get her away from her late husband's brother, whom Aisha's widowed mother was compelled to marry, and who has begun showing a lecherous interest in his adopted daughter.

Aisha's mother has her daughter's wrist tattooed with a cross in order to pass her off as a Christian and brings her to an English-speaking convent school in Assiut, where she begs the nuns to let her daughter in as a charity student. Aisha (passed off as "Mary") thus begins a life far different from her previous one, although she is forced to leave the school after a few years, when a scandal erupts involving one of the nuns. With nowhere to go, Aisha turns in desperation to a wealthy classmate, which improbably leads her to meet a young Howard Carter, future discoverer of the tomb of Tutankhamun. Carter is immediately taken by Aisha's resemblance to the pharaonic paintings he sketches as part of his work.

The novel provides an affectionate portrait of life in the Sa'id, as well as some gorgeous descriptions of the natural environment, which blend seamlessly with the rest of the narrative. Early on, for example, Qandil compares the irrigation canals that branch off from the Nile to "veins of the body, blood red at the time of the floods, while the earth is black as musk, the crops as green as emerald, the wheat as yellow as jasper stone".

Zelig-like, Aisha is brought to the attention of the unpleasant Lord Cromer and hired on as a lady-in-waiting to his wife. Aisha soon becomes the family interpreter, and translates an awkward, politically charged conversation between Lady Cromer and the intellectual Princess Nazli Fazil. She also translates for Cromer the scathing newspaper headlines that followed the brutal Dinshaway incident, which (in both real life and in the novel) led to his removal after protests from Egyptian nationalists in 1907.

Mohamed Mansi Qandil

Unhappy with the Cromers, Aisha falls in with the young nationalist leader Mustafa Kamil and becomes the first female employee
of his party's newspaper, al-Liwa'. She also has a failed love affair
with the budding young sculptor Mahmoud Mukhtar. Her happy
life in Cairo is interrupted by the arrival of her uncle, who has
tracked her down in Cairo and deceives her into returning to her

village, only to hold her prisoner and brutally rape her before she can escape back to Cairo.

Qandil's novel is shot through with fine observations on the relations between colonizing Europeans and the peasants of the Sa'id they encounter in Luxor, particularly in the hostile relationship between Carter and a local grave-robber who caters to the growing market in stolen antiquities. Avoiding the pitfalls of many historical novels, Qandil's characters for the most part feel like genuine characters rather than mouthpieces.

Unusually, the novel switches perspectives several times during the course of the book from Aisha to Carter, letting him speak as a first-person narrator. By contrast, when the narrative focuses on Aisha, she never speaks in the first person: it seems like a missed opportunity. Additionally, late in the novel the narrative shifts to ancient Egypt, focusing on Akhenaten's tenuous religious and political revolution against the priests of Luxor. Later, the young Tutankhamun ascends the throne as a weak young ruler under the thumb of the general Horemheb, helpless to stop the overthrow of Akhenaten's monotheistic Aten-worship and the restoration of the old pantheon. The final chapters shift back and forth between Tutankhamun's story and the narrative of Carter and Aisha as they close in on the discovery of his tomb in 1922.

Aisha's ability to reshape herself to accommodate the changing circumstances in which she finds herself – from Sa'idi village girl to convent-school student, Egyptologist, interpreter, and journalist – can be read as a metaphor for the experience of the colonization. The novel works best when it conveys Aisha's reversals of fortunes through protectorate-era Egypt, but by the end of the novel, she seems to drop out as a character. As Howard and his workmen grow closer to uncovering Tutankhamun's lost tomb, Aisha retreats to their shared house on the western bank, where she is eventually killed by the wolves that have menaced all the characters over the course of the novel, a recurring symbol of menace and death on the western shore of the Nile, the symbolic Land of the Dead. Still, in Barbara Romaine's masterful translation, *A Cloudy Day on the Western Shore* presents an engaging portrait of a young Sa'idi woman rising through society and an enjoyable overview of early 20th-century Egypt.

Hannah Somerville reviews

In the Spider's Room
by Muhammad Abdelnabi

Translated by Jonathan Wright

Hoopoe Fiction (AUC Press, July 2018)
ISBN 978-9774168758. Pbk, 224pp, £9.99 / USD 16.95

When the truth remains opaque

To read Muhammad Abdelnabi's latest fictional offering is to experience a measure of disquiet. This has nothing to do with the subject matter: *In the Spider's Room* is a frank, un-abashedly tender exposition of male homosexuality in Cairo, albeit one received through a distorting mesh of tears and hyperbole, but it is not a "difficult" read. Nor is it to do with the novel's disrupted chronology, its effortless but at times dizzying intertext, or the occasional sense of being clobbered over the head by extended metaphor. Rather it is because, at the close, the reader is compelled to decide how far and why we, too, have been "strung along".

We should expect nothing less from Abdelnabi, who since 2009 has run a weekly workshop, The Story and What's In It, on storycraft and narrative technique, and has expressed a preoccupation with the fraught boundaries between reality and its narration. As well as his English-to-Arabic translation credits, he has penned two novels, a novella, and two short story collections, *The Ghost of Anton Chekhov* (2009) winning the Sawiris Cultural Award (Short Story) of 2010. *In the Spider's Room* (Al-Ain Publishing, Cairo, 2016) was shortlisted for the 2017 International Prize for Arabic Fiction and in January this year won the 2017 Sawiris Award for Best Novel of an Emerging Writer. The English edition comes to us courtesy of Hoopoe and the distinguished Jonathan Wright, buoyed along, in effect, by the sort of externally legitimising forces the novel's queasy narrator

would no doubt be grateful for.

In broad strokes, *In the Spider's Room* takes as its point of departure the notorious Queen Boat affair of 2001, in which vice squad and security forces raided a floating nightclub moored on the Nile, arresting 52 men, fifty being charged with "habitual debauchery" and "obscene behaviour", and two with "contempt of religion". Their trials lasted over a year, during which they were incarcerated in prison, enduring beatings, degrading "forensic examinations", and continual vilification in the Egyptian media. The second trial ended in March 2003, sentencing 21 to three-year terms and acquitting the other 29.

The fictional trajectory of Hani Mahfouz, a peripheral figure rounded up in the streets along with his lover Abdel Aziz during the police raids, is the focus of Abdelnabi's novel. Freshly released from prison, the traumatised Hani has lost the power of speech, and with the web of lies constituting his old life now torn apart, he contrives, gingerly, to re-write his story.

The coming-of-age tale emerges in a series of carefully curated vignettes and flashbacks, imbued with thoughtful descriptive elements that lend a sense of authenticity to proceedings – if not quite realism. In Hani's retelling of his acting/dressmaking family, in the minutiae of gesture and material accoutrement scattered in the portrayal of his Margot Channing-like mother, one can trace the vacillations of Egyptian society's social and material fortunes over the decades. And the character's forays into Cairo's underground gay scene serve as an important, earnest testimony to the variety of lived queer experience in this city. For Hani at least, it plays out in furtive nods and meetings of eyes, in forceful encounters on dusty workshop floors, in hotel roof gardens and working-class Turkish baths, enacted by everyone from chain-smoking youths that "play the game" with flaneur-like detachment to ageing, perfume-doused godfather figures such as the only mildly preposterous "Prince Aktham".

In this and other matters, Abdelnabi has done his research. The passages pertaining to the Queen Boat tragedy defer extensively to events as they were reported at the time: a cursory glance at Human Rights Watch documentation reveals the extent to which some of the men's testimonies have been reproduced almost verbatim in In the Spider's Room. The obsessive mandate of medical officers: "Active or passive?", the degrading physical treatment of the "Cairo 52" and the catastrophic injury to their families all echo in Hani's recollections of Tora prison. But there are also flashes of solace, and of human comradeship. Among the memorable protagonists is Hani's cellmate Karim, a refreshingly abstruse Azhari scholar and self-confessed "Child of Lot", who at the narrator's behest enacts a literal version of what is really the novel's core vocation: he tells stories in order to make prison bearable.

The work's fatal flaw lies in its designated tale-teller. The narrator is both insufferable and wilfully obfuscating, rationalising the novel's every encounter in reductive, quasi-Freudian terms. The result is a semi-obscured reconstruction of events in which performativity, cynicism and manipulation emerge as privileged themes. Over and over Hani re-invents himself, from the outrageous queen "Hanushka" to "circus performer" in a singularly cruel sham marriage, and his amorous pursuits, up to and including that of the ambiguous Abdel Aziz, come tinged either with ineffable campiness or abject nihilism. Worse, he warms unstoppably to his hackneyed showbiz theme, and each twist comes wrapped in an exhaustive, exhausting web of thespian metaphor: masks, dramas, stages, denuded myths. In this particular spider's room, fascinating protagonists and potential doors to understanding lead a half-life as fleeting props for Hani's last stab at re-invention.

That said, this is a far from unrewarding read. It is illuminating in many ways, and devoid of any overtly allegorical characters. Among the more repetitive motifs Abdelnabi deploys some haunting, evocative turns of phrase: "a joy as fragile as an April fool's joke" passes over a face, and the false hope of unrequited love is "a disfigured child, born old and malevolent . . . strewing possibilities and hy-

Muhammad Abdelnabi, Abu Dhabi Book Fair 2017, photo by Samuel Shimon

potheses". Moreover, it reads very well in translation, with the smoothness and easy domestication of colloquial terms we can expect from Jonathan Wright.

If *In the Spider's Room* has any indisputable wisdom to impart, it is this: don't trust the cover. This is not a fictional prison memoir, nor a story of true love, as the English-language blurb and illustrations imply. Instead, of its early reviews I am inclined to agree with one blogger's bitter contention that it emerges as a parable of internalised homophobia: a prison memoir, arguably, but of another kind. If this has been achieved reflexively by Abdelnabi's design, then it is a masterful work of literature. If by accident, it is cause for great melancholy. But as with so many other elements of this novel, its truth remains opaque.

Aldo Nicosia reviews

Al-Digla fi 'Arajiniha

(Dates on their branches)

by Béchir Khraief

New edition published by Dar Al Janub,
Tunis, 2000.

Mines, men
and dates

As I introduce *Al-Digla fi 'Arajiniha* (Dates on their branches, 1969), by Béchir Khraief (also Al-Bashir Khurayyif), a short story by Tayeb Salih pops into my mind – *Hafnat Tamr* (*A Handful of Dates*). Both the novel and the short story share the date palm as a key aesthetic referent in an environment of greediness, violence but also self-cultivation. Salih, impressed by several similarities between his Sudan, and the Tunisian world represented in the novel, wrote a rhapsodic preface to it.

Khraief chooses as the novel's main setting his birthplace, Nefta, along with other places in southwestern Tunisia, the Djerid region. This was an area of resistance and rebellion against the French colonizers and, after Independence in 1956, against the Tunisian governments. Its collective memory is still influenced by those important times. The events of the novel span two decades, 1910 to 1930, when outstanding intellectuals such as Tahar Haddad and the "national poet" Abu al-Qasim al-Shabbi, both born and raised in Tunisia's deep south, were leaving their indelible influence on Tunisian society.

Since the 19th century revolts, lead by Ali Ben Ghedhahem (1814–1867) and sung by oral poetry, until the recent uprisings of January 2008 in Redeyef, the entire Gafsa mining area has repeatedly been the scene of protests against unemployment, low wages and unfair recruitment.

The novel is divided into three parts, called *'arajin*, the same

Béchir Khraief

branches of the date palm of its title. Each is named after its main character, respectively Dija (the local diminutive of Khadija), Mekki and 'Atra.

In the first, the divorced Dija is living in the care of her kind brother Muldi, whereas the older sibling, Haffa, has taken control of Dija's share of the family palm grove.

Dija's son Mekki, despite his parents' separation, spends a happy childhood with little cousins Larbi and 'Atra, Muldi's sons. When their parents die, they also shift under the protection of Aunt Dija. She would like to go back to her husband but does not dare to go against Haffa's plans. Struck down by hemiplegia, she dies.

Years go by, Larbi volunteers for the French army, while Mekki attends school in Nefta and then escapes to Metlawi, which has been turned into a big phosphate mining centre, attracting workers from even Italy, Malta and Greece. He gets a job there as a storekeeper.

In the second part, Mekki is involved in the miners' struggle against the colonizers, together with the leader Dabanjaq, who is based on the real Mohamed Ali El-Hammi (1890-1928), who

عيون المعاصرة

السير غيري

الزّقلة في عراجينها

تقديم
الطيب صالح

دار الجنوب
Collection : Mohamed HAMDANE

founded the first Arab union trade, the General Federation of Tunisian Workers, in 1924. Mekki organizes evening classes to educate his fellow workers, and then a general strike. All that happens in November 1928 – the French army intervenes heavily and many are killed or jailed in the capital. Thwarted by the failure of his nationalist dreams, Mekki is not even able to find consolation with prostitutes. Infected with a venereal disease, he decides to go back to his village.

In the third part, Haffa forces 'Atra to marry his cousin Mekki when he realises Mekki is about to die. 'Atra is then married off to her cousin Hafnawi. Travelling back from Sfax, where 'Atra was cured of a toothache, Hafnawi has a strange quarrel with the conductor and has to leave the train. At Gafsa railway station 'Atra runs into Gharsa, a prostitute, who invites her to her friends' house. There she spends a crazy night with an unknown lover. Meanwhile, the husband marries a second wife, and then 'Atra dies of consumption.

The novel can be seen in the tradition of a naturalism reinforced by the use of direct, unadorned language: all dialogue is in the southern Tunisian dialect, and that has been the source of vehement debates in the local cultural scene. It can be also regarded as a sociological document about a forgotten part of Tunisia, whose spaces and characters are described with a refined sense of humour and irony. Khraief convinces the reader that he truly belongs to that world, with all its tragic misery, hypocrisy, vices and virtues. In his preface, Salih stresses that the novel "has the Shakespearean power to mix the comic with the serious". To date only a French translation is available for non-Arabic readers (*La terre des passions brulées*, translated by Hédi Djebnoun and Assia Djebar, J.-C. Lattes, 1986), but it has so many cuts and deletions as to be unacceptable. As a 3D projection of a socio-political reality, not completely out of date, this work really deserves to be translated into other languages, at least out of respect for the author's contribution to modern Arabic literature.

Clare Roberts reviews four novels

Outclassed in Kuwait
by Taleb Alrefai

Cigarette Number Seven
by Donia Kamal

One Syrian Summer
by Dorothy Al Khafaji

A Morocco Anthology,
edited by Martin Rose

Outclassed in Kuwait
by Taleb Alrefai

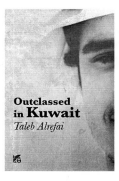

Outclassed in **Kuwait**
Taleb Alrefai

In this rather extraordinary short novel a successful but by no means wealthy author is taken aback when faced with the proposition of writing a biographical novel about a successful Kuwaiti businessman for a large sum of money. Full of doubts but enticed by the financial reward on offer, he is warned that he will not be able to write about the private life of the businessman, focusing exclusively on his professional rise to success. In particular, he is told, he must not include any details about the life of his wife and her family. But the more time he spends with the businessman in order for him to recount his life story, the more the writer realises that the personal cannot be extricated from the professional quite so easily. It also becomes clear that there are many people vehemently opposed to this project, and the writer realises that there is perhaps some truth to the old adage that "water doesn't mix with oil, even if it's in the same pot". Family ties, social mobility, artistic integrity and the crippling fear of scandal are recurring themes. This is a short but thought-provoking read that sheds an interesting light on Kuwaiti high society, power and politics. Hamad bin Khalifa University Press, Qatar, 2018. ISBN 9789927119385. Pbk, 146pp. Also E-Book.

Cigarette Number Seven
by Donia Kamal

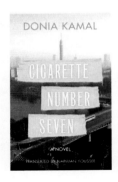

In this novel, Donia Kamal's second, the events of the Egyptian revolution of 2011 unfold through the eyes of a young female protagonist. Relationships with men – particularly her activist father and the various men to whom she has formed romantic attachments – form an important part of this story, in which the protagonist also tries to come to terms with her fear of death, her inability to settle and memories from a difficult childhood during which her mother left Egypt in order to seek work in the Gulf. The novel illustrates a unique moment in recent Egyptian history, a period characterised, in the eyes of this protagonist, by demonstrations, passion, romantic ideals and instability. The novel will be of particular interest for those seeking to understand how the revolution unfolded in Tahrir Square during that pivotal period. Written in a simple, frank style and translated by Nariman Youssef, this novel represents, perhaps, Kamal's attempts to document some of her own memories from 2011. Hoopoe Fiction, Egypt, December 2017. ISBN: 9789774168505. Pbk, 224pp, $17.95 / £9.99 / LE200. https://hoopoefiction.com/ book/cigarette-number-seven/

One Syrian Summer
by Dorothy Al Khafaji

This new novel by Dorothy Al Khafaji explores the lives of an Iraqi family and their friends as they become embroiled in the complexities of aid work in neighbouring Syria, humanitarian relief efforts in Yemen, and the familial concerns and complications such developments inevitably cause generally for the family. When Omar and his friends make the somewhat rash decision to help as aid workers in Syria over a summer holiday, they quickly realise their naiveté, as they get sucked into the conflict and pulled in different directions by ISIS, the Free Syrian Army and the Syrian Mukhabarat. In such perilous circumstances, and often going to dangerous extremes to help protect everyday Syrians caught up in the conflict, the boys are never far from danger. But even Omar's sister Alia, back in Baghdad, suffers as a result of her brother's decision when she is blackmailed into becoming a double agent. Meanwhile, their sister Lena embarks upon difficult medical work in Yemen, where she is forced to make some heartbreaking medical choices. With all of this to contend with, parents who have long been distant from one another are forced to come together for the sake of their children. The novel offers a very human face to life inside Middle Eastern conflict zones, through the eyes of people who, despite always seeking to do good, do not necessarily always make good decisions. A touching story of humanitarian work, romance and the power of family ties. The Book Guild Ltd, UK, July 2018. ISBN 9781912362936. Pbk, 243pp, £8.99 / USD10.38. https://www.bookguild.co.uk/bookshop-collection/fiction/one-syrian-summer/

A Morocco Anthology: Travel Writing through the Centuries, edited by Martin Rose

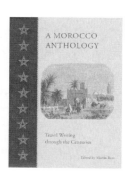

In this short anthology, former director of the British Council in Morocco, Martin Rose, has curated a beautiful collection of some of the scenes, sites and stories that have made, and continue to make, Morocco such a fascinating place to visit. Focusing particularly on the cities of Fes, Marrakech, Essouira, Meknes, Rabat and Tangier, the anthology brings together extracts from some of the most famous travel writers and explorers of this region from the 17th century to the present day. From the palpable "pang of regret" one feels when leaving Essouira's "perfect climate" to the rather gory custom of pickling the heads of the sultan's enemies in Rabat; from the lost libraries of Fes to Sultan Abdel Aziz's yearning for a toy railway, there is something to please every type of reader in this delightful collection of anecdotes. American University in Cairo Press, Egypt, 2018. ISBN 9789774168468. Hbk, 160pp. £11.99 / USD18.95. http://www.britishmoroccansociety.org/a-morocco-anthology/

FICTION AND POETRY

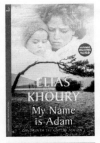

My Name is Adam. Children of the Ghetto, Volume I, by Elias Khoury. Adam Dannoun discovers he is not who he thinks he is, and sets out to investigate exactly happened in 1948 in Palestine in the city of Lydda. Translated from the Arabic by Humphrey Davies. MacLehose Press, October 2018. ISBN: 9780857057518, Pbk, 448pp, £16. Ebook: ISBN:9780857057501

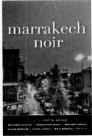

Marrakech Noir ed Yassin Adnan. Brand-new stories by fifteen Moroccan writers. Translated from Arabic, Ffrench and Dutch. Publisher: Akashic Noir Series, : Akashic Books (August 7, 2018) ISBN-13: 978-1617754739. Pbk, 256 pp. $15.95 / £11.99

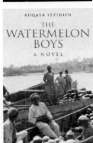

The Watermelon Boys by Ruqaya Izzidien. The paths of two teenage boys, Ahmed from Iraq and Welsh Carwyn cross in WWI's Mesopotamian campaign. Hoopoe Fiction, 30 August 2018. ISBN: 978-9774168802, Pbk, 264pp, $17.95 / £9.99.

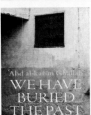

We have Buried the Past by Moroccan author and journalist Abd al-karim Ghallab. First published in Arabic in 1966, this postcolonial novel follows a patriarchal family struggling with 20th century social change. Haus Publishing, October 2018. Translated by Roger Allen. ISBN: 9781910376409. Pbk, 352pp, £12.99

By Moroccan film-maker and author Ahmed Bouanani (1938–2011)
The Hospital. A haunting and hallucinatory tale, first published in 1989 and based on Bouanani's own experiences as a tuberculosis patient. Translated from the French by Lara Vergnaud. New Directions, June 2018. ISBN: 978-0811225762. NDP1411. Pbk, 128pp. $14.95 / £10.99

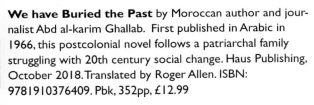

The Shutters. This poetry collection by Ahmed Bouanani reconstructs vivid images of Morocco's past, including its "years of lead". Translated from the French by Emma Ramadan. New Directions, NDP1410. July 2018. ISBN: 978-0811227841. Pbk, 172pp, $16.95 /£10.99

NON-FICTION

The Arab Renaissance: A Bilingual Anthology of the Nahda, ed. Tarek El-Ariss. Texts by intellectuals, writers, clergy, and political figures that deal with authority, social norms, conventions and practices both secular and religious, gender roles, class, travel, and technology. Pub. MLA (MLA Texts and Translations Series), 2018. ISBN: 9781603293037. 448 pp, pbk, $22.

Kamel Daoud Chroniques: Selected columns 2012-16. Translated by Elisabeth Zerofsky, Other Press, October 2018. ISBN: 9781590519561. Hbk, 336pp, £24.99. E-book £16.79.

An Introduction to Modern Arab Culture by Bassam Frangieh. Cognella Academic Publishing, August 2018. ISBN: 978-1-5165-2629-1. Pbk, 434pp. $107.95 / £83.25.

New Geographies: Texts and Contexts in Modern Arabic Literature edited by Roger Allen, Gonzalo Fernández Parrilla, F M Rodríguez, Tetz Rooke. Papers of the EURAMAL Conference 2014. Autonomous University of Madrid, 2018. ISBN: 9788483446201. Pbk, 296pp, €25.

Islam and the Culture of Modern Egypt: From the Monarchy to the Republic, by Mohammad Salama. Cambridge University Press, November 2018. ISBN: 978-11082650-2-7. Hbk, £75.00.

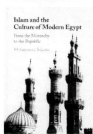

The Culinary Crescent: A History of Middle Eastern Cuisine by Peter Heine. Translated by Peter Lewis.

ISBN:978-1-909942-25-7. Hbk, 235pp, £30/$44.95.

FEAST: Food of the Islamic World by Anissa Helou. Bloomsbury, October 2018. ISBN:9781526602862. Hbk, 544pp, illustrated, £45/$44.95.

Assilah 2018

This year the Assilah Cultural Festival celebrated its 40th year of filling the small Atlantic coast town every summer with poetry, concerts, murals, dance, workshops, performance, numerous panels on cultural and social subjects, with hundreds of Arab and foreign guests, writers, performers, artists and dignitaries from around the world. Senegal's President Macky Sall was one of a number of African leaders to be welcomed since the Festival's Guest of Honour on this special 40th session was Africa itself. The Festival activities are occasions for unfettered dialogue and international friendships, nurtured by generations for 40 years.

In addition to the daily programme, the Festival awards three prizes in memory of major writers who participated in the Assilah Festival themselves over many years. Congolese writer and poet

Amadou Lamine Sall, winner of the Tchicaya U Tams'si Prize for African Poetry

Tchicaya U Tams'si first visited in 1981, and then every year until his death in 1989. The biennial Tchicaya U Tams'si Prize for African Poetry was awarded this year to Amadou Lamine Sall from Senegal. A major award-winning francophone African poet who was considered by Léopold Sédar Senghor as one of "the most gifted poet of his generation", Sall is founder of the African House of International Poetry and author of more than 15 collections of poetry, many translated into several languages.

The Mohamed Zafzaf Prize for the Novel was this year awarded to Ahmed El Madini, Moroccan novelist, literary critic and researcher. He has written eight novels, eight short story collections,

Ahmed El Madini (centre), receives his awarrd of the Mohamed Zafzaf Prize for the Novel from chair of jury Rashid al-Uraimi (left) and Mohamed Benaissa, Secretary General of the Assilah Forum Foundation

Mohamed El Arbi and Nassima Raoui, winners of the Buland al-Haidari Poetry Prize

four poetry collections and numerous scholarly texts and literary studies. His complete works, in five volumes, were published by the Moroccan Ministry of Culture in 2014. Mohamed Zafzaf (1942–2001), one of Morocco's best-known and loved authors, published his first novel when he was 35, pioneering an innovative and modern aesthetic that described lived realities and the world of the marginalized rooted in the daily anxieties of ordinary man.

The third of the Festival's prizes is the Buland al-Haidari Prize for young Arab Poetry. Iraqi Kurdish poet Buland al-Haidari (1926–1996) lived and died in exile. He deemed personal and daily life worthy of a poet's attention and revolutionized Arabic poetry by writing on these themes in free verse. This year there were two winners, both of them giving inspired readings of their works to the Moussem audience at the award ceremony. Nassima Raoui (b. 1988) is a poet and novelist from Rabat. She has two collections of poetry and a novel, as well as works published in anthologies. Mohamed El Arbi, originally from Nabeul in northeast Tunisia, was the other winner. He has published poems, short stories and articles in national and Arabic newspapers and magazines and was awarded the

President Macky Sall of Senegal   Mário Lúcio from Cape Verde

2014 Tunisian House of Poetry Prize. Selected poems are translated into French, English, Persian and Kurdish.

Many of the concerts take place in the beautiful Palace of Culture. This year there was a performance by Mário Lúcio, singer, composer, writer, politician and painter from Cape Verde, who was the country's Minister of Culture 2011–2016. Also inside Assilah's walled medina is the Hassan II Centre for International Meetings hosting debates and exhibitions. Its gallery hosted a photographic and poster exhibition on the life of Léopold Sédar Senghor (1906–2001), in collaboration with the Léopold Sédar Senghor Foundation.

In tandem with the arts and musical events, the Assilah Forum initiates and hosts two and three-day debates on current hot topics, often taking place in the auditorium of the modern Prince Bandar Bin Sultan Library. This year the subjects were: "Religious Thought that nurtures Terrorism: Its intellectual origins and how to confront it"; "After Globalisation, What Next?"; and "The Safeguard and Transmission of Music in the Islamic World", drawing in experts, researchers, critics and literary and political figures from the Arab and African worlds and beyond.

Alfonso Armada is a journlist, chronicler, and poet, born in Vigo in 1958. He has worked for the newspapers *El País* (he covered Sarajevo and was a correspondent in Africa) and *ABC* (for which he was a correspondent in NY and Director of the Masters in Journalism). He lives in Madrid.

Salah Awad is an Iraqi poet and journalist, born in 1956 in Baghdad. He left Iraq in 1979 and in 1988 settled in the USA. He has two poetry collections and his work is published in several anthologies. He is a journalist at the UN in New York.

Adil Babikir is a Sudanese translator into and out of English & Arabic, living now in Abu Dhabi. He has translated *Mansi: a Rare Man in his Own Way* by Tayeb Salih, forthcoming in 2019 from Banipal Books, and two novels by Abdelaziz Baraka Sakin. Other translations include two anthologies – of poetry and short stories.

Fadhil Chalabi was born in Baghdad in 1929. He was an oil economist, serving in the Iraqi oil Ministry. He was Acting Secretary General of OPEC 1983–1988, and then Executive Director of the Centre for Global Energy Studies 1987–2011 until his retirement.

Raphael Cohen is a translator based in Cairo and a contributing editor of Banipal. His recent Arabic fiction translations include Mona Prince's *So You May See* (2011) & Status: Emo by *Eslam Mosbah*. He is a contributing editor of *Banipal*.

Ahmed Salah Eldein is an Egyptian writer and translator of Russian to Arabic born in Cairo in 1973. He published his first book *Heirs of Tolstoy on Kosnitsky Bridge* in 2015 – a portrait of the contemporary Russian literary scene in Arabic. His translation of Nobel Laureate Svetlana Alexievich's *Chernobyl Prayer* (2016) gained instant success and became a bestseller. He studied English language and literature at Ain Shams University and Russian language and literature at Ruden University in Moscow (Patrice Lumumba).

Najlaa Eltom is a Sudanese writer and translator. Her work includes poetry, short story, literary essay and commentary, with some translated into English and Swedish. She contributed to the translation of several Sudanese literary texts into

English, including the winner of the Caine Prize, 2017. She moved to Sweden in 2012.

Bassam Frangieh is a professor of Arabic at Claremont McKenna College and a scholar of contemporary Arabic literature and culture. He previously taught at Georgetown University and Yale University. His books include *An Introduction to Modern Arab Culture* and *Anthology of Arabic Literature, Culture and Thought: From Pre-Islamic Times to the Present*. He has translated the works of several leading Arab poets and novelists into English, including *Arabian Love Poems* of Nizar Qabbani, *Love, Death and Exile*, poems of Abdel Wahab al-Bayati, *The Crane* by Halim Barakat and *Sun On A Cloudy Day* by Hanna Mina. He is a consulting editor of *Banipal*.

Peter Kalu is a writer and editor, based in Manchester, UK. He has nine published novels, ranging from science fiction to romantic comedy, plus radio and theatre plays. He was a translator of commercial French into English before joining the new writing development agency Commonword/ Cultureword, becoming their Artistic Director in 2008, and convenor of the UK National Black Writers Conference every two years. He was a judge on the 2017 Saif Ghobash Banipal Prize for Arabic Literary Translation.

Becki Maddock is a translator and researcher living in London. She translates from Arabic, Persian and Spanish into English. She has a first class BA in Arabic and Spanish (Exeter University) and an MA in Near and Middle Eastern Studies from SOAS, University of London. She is taking Kurdish language classes, also at SOAS.

Ahmed Morsi see pages 80–86

Aldo Nicosia, a teacher of Arabic language and literature at the University of Bari, Italy, has published several essays and articles about Arab cinema, translation studies and dialectology.

Ruth Padel is is an award-winning British poet, Professor of Poetry at King's College, London, with close links to Greece, music and conservation. She has published eleven poetry collections, shortlisted for all major UK prizes. They include *Darwin – A Life in Poems*, a verse biography of her great-great grandfather Charles Darwin; *The Mara Crossing* on human and animal migration; *Learning to Make an Oud in Nazareth*, on the Middle East; *Tidings*, a narrative poem on homelessness and Christmas, and most recently *Emerald*, an elegy for her 97-year-old mother.

Azza Rashad was born in Al-Sharqiya province of Egypt in 1961, and graduated in medicine and surgery, specialising in paediatrics and working in Health Ministry hospitals. Her debut novel, *Memory of Wilderness*, was published in 2003 (Merit). She has three short story collections, *Girls of my Dreams*, *Half Light* and *I love Nura, I hate Nurhan*.

Clare Roberts has a BA in Arabic and Islamic Studies from Oxford University, and an MA in Arabic Poetry and Turkish Politics from SOAS, Londo). She works at Gingko Library and is a contributing editor of *Banipal* and a regular reviewer.

Chip Rosetti has translated several works of Arabic fiction, including *Beirut, Beirut* by Sonallah Ibrahim, *Utopia* by Ahmed Khaled Towfik, and the graphic novel *Metro* by Magdy El Shafee. He is Editorial Director of the Library of Arabic Literature book series at NYU Press. He has a doctorate in Arabic literature from the University of Pennsylvania.

Mekkawi Said lived his whole life in Cairo, where he was born. He was a publisher, script writer and regular contributor to children's magazines, and has five collections of short stories, his first pub-

CONTRIBUTORS

lished in 1981. His first novel won him the Suad Sabbah Arab Creativity Prize in 1991, and in 2008 he was awarded the Egyptian State Prize for Literature. His second, *Cairo Swan Song*, was shortlisted for the inaugural International Prize for Arabic Fiction in 2008, and later published by AUC Press in English translation by Adam Talib.

Balkis Sharara is an author, sister of Hayat Sharara, and wife of renowned Iraqi architect Rifat Chadirji. In 1979 she carried copies of his works into and out of Abu Ghraib allowing him to author three of his seminal books while in the prison. On his release they wrote a book of their experiences, *A Wall Between Two Darknesses* (2003), reviewed in *Banipal 24*.

Hayat Sharara – see pages 12–28

Girgis Shukry was born in Sohag, Egypt, on 27 August 1967. He has six collections of poetry. He has read his works at many international poetry festivals and has poems translated into Dutch, French, German and English. In 2001 he participated in the Swiss-Egyptian New Writings project in Cairo, and a volume of his selected poems was published in a German edition in 2004 (Sabon Verlag, Switzerland). He is a journalist on cultural affairs for Cairo's radio and TV magazine.

Hannah Somerville is a London-based investigative journalist and former health reporter. She has a BA in Arabic and Spanish from the University of Leeds and an MA in Arabic Literature from SOAS, University of London. Her dissertation focused on body politics in new Egyptian 'dystopian' fiction.

Paul Starkey is Emeritus Professor of Ara-

bic at Durham University and Vice-President of BRISMES. He has translated many works by contemporary Arab authors, and won the 2015 Saif Ghobash Banipal Prize for Youssef Rakha's *The Book of the Sultan's Seal* (Interlink, 2014). He is a contributing editor of *Banipal* and chair of the Banipal Trust.

Bill Swainson is a literary consultant and freelance editor, working as Consultant Editor for Fiction at MacLehose Press and Editor at Large for Non-fiction at Oneworld. He also edits books for a wide range of publishers including Alma, Canongate, Haus Publishing and the Gingko Library, and consults for the French Institute, Trinity Centre for Literary Translation in Dublin and the Santa Maddalena Foundation in Italy.

Susannah Tarbush is a freelance journalist specialising in cultural affairs in the Middle East. She writes the Tanjara blog, and is a consulting editor of *Banipal* and regular reviewer.

Valentina Viene is Italian by birth, now settled in the UK. She has a BA degree in Arabic and English from the University of Naples L'Orientale, and an MA in the Theory and Practice of Arabic Translation.

Jonathan Wright is an award-winning translator whose translations include three IPAF winners, Ahmed Saadawi's *Frankenstein in Baghdad* (IPAF 2014), Saud Alsanousi's *The Bamboo Stalk* (IPAF 2013) for which he won for the 2016 Saif Ghobash Banipal Prize), and Youssef Ziedan's *Azazeel* (IPAF 2009) which was joint winner of the 2013 Saif Ghobash Banipal Prize). His translation of Hassan Blasim's *The Iraqi Christ* won the 2014 Independent Foreign Fiction Prize.

For more information on all the authors in *Banipal 63* and all the translators, writers and book reviewers, please go to:
www.banipal.co.uk/contributors/